Love, Life & Work

Being a Book of Opinions Reasonably Good-Natured Concerning How to Attain the Highest Happiness for One's Self with the Least Possible Harm to Others

Love, Life & Work

Being a Book of Opinions Reasonably Good-Natured Concerning How to Attain the Highest Happiness for One's Self with the Least Possible Harm to Others

ELBERT HUBBARD

ROCKVILLE, MARYLAND
2009

Love, Life & Work, Being a Book of Opinions Reasonably Good-Natured Concerning How to Attain the Highest Happiness for One's Self with the Least Possible Harm to Others by **Elbert Hubbard** in its current format, copyright © Serenity Publishers 2009. This book, in whole or in part, may not be copied or reproduced in its current format by any means, electronic, mechanical or otherwise without the permission of the publisher.

The original text has been reformatted for clarity and to fit this edition.

Serenity Publishers & associated logos are trademarks or registered trademarks of Serenity Publishers, Rockville, Maryland. All other trademarks are properties of their respective owners.

This book is presented as is, without any warranties (implied or otherwise) as to the accuracy of the production, text or translation. The publisher does not take responsibility for any typesetting, formatting, translation or other errors which may have occurred during the production of this book.

ISBN: 978-1-60450-572-6

Published by Serenity Publishers
An Arc Manor Company
P. O. Box 10339
Rockville, MD 20849-0339
www.SerenityPublishers.com
Printed in the United States of America/United Kingdom

Contents

1.	A PRAYER	7
2.	LIFE AND EXPRESSION	8
3.	TIME AND CHANCE	13
4.	PSYCHOLOGY OF A RELIGIOUS REVIVAL	16
5.	ONE-MAN POWER	28
6.	MENTAL ATTITUDE	31
7.	THE OUTSIDER	34
8.	GET OUT OR GET IN LINE	38
9.	THE WEEK-DAY, KEEP IT HOLY	44
10.	EXCLUSIVE FRIENDSHIPS	48
11.	THE FOLLY OF LIVING IN THE FUTURE	53
12.	THE SPIRIT OF MAN	55
13.	ART AND RELIGION	58

14.	INITIATIVE	63
15.	THE DISAGREEABLE GIRL	64
16.	THE NEUTRAL	69
17.	REFLECTIONS ON PROGRESS	71
18.	SYMPATHY, KNOWLEDGE AND POISE	78
19.	LOVE AND FAITH	81
20.	GIVING SOMETHING FOR NOTHING	83
21.	WORK AND WASTE	87
22.	THE LAW OF OBEDIENCE	89
23.	SOCIETY'S SAVIORS	91
24.	PREPARING FOR OLD AGE	93
25.	AN ALLIANCE WITH NATURE	98
26.	THE EX. QUESTION	102
27.	THE SERGEANT	108
28.	THE SPIRIT OF THE AGE	112
29.	THE GRAMMARIAN	115
30.	THE BEST RELIGION	118

A Prayer

The supreme prayer of my heart is not to be learned, rich, famous, powerful, or "good," but simply to be radiant. I desire to radiate health, cheerfulness, calm courage and good will. I wish to live without hate, whim, jealousy, envy, fear. I wish to be simple, honest, frank, natural, clean in mind and clean in body, unaffected—ready to say "I do not know," if it be so, and to meet all men on an absolute equality—to face any obstacle and meet every difficulty unabashed and unafraid.

I wish others to live their lives, too—up to their highest, fullest and best. To that end I pray that I may never meddle, interfere, dictate, give advice that is not wanted, or assist when my services are not needed. If I can help people, I'll do it by giving them a chance to help themselves; and if I can uplift or inspire, let it be by example, inference, and suggestion, rather than by injunction and dictation. That is to say, I desire to be radiant—to radiate life.

LIFE AND EXPRESSION

By exercise of its faculties the spirit grows, just as a muscle grows strong thru continued use. Expression is necessary. Life is expression, and repression is stagnation—death.

Yet, there can be right and wrong expression. If a man permits his life to run riot and only the animal side of his nature is allowed to express itself, he is repressing his highest and best, and the qualities not used atrophy and die.

Men are punished by their sins, not for them. Sensuality, gluttony, and the life of license repress the life of the spirit, and the soul never blossoms; and this is what it is to lose one's soul. All adown the centuries thinking men have noted these truths, and again and again we find individuals forsaking in horror the life of the senses and devoting themselves to the life of the spirit. This question of expression through the spirit, or through the senses—through soul or body—

has been the pivotal point of all philosophy and the inspiration of all religion.

Every religion is made up of two elements that never mix any more than oil and water mix. A religion is a mechanical mixture, not a chemical combination, of morality and dogma. Dogma is the science of the unseen: the doctrine of the unknown and unknowable. And in order to give this science plausibility, its promulgators have always fastened upon it morality. Morality can and does exist entirely separate and apart from dogma, but dogma is ever a parasite on morality, and the business of the priest is to confuse the two.

But morality and religion never saponify. Morality is simply the question of expressing your life forces—how to use them? You have so much energy; and what will you do with it? And from out the multitude there have always been men to step forward and give you advice for a consideration. Without their supposed influence with the unseen we might not accept their interpretation of what is right and wrong. But with the assurance that their advice is backed up by Deity, followed with an offer of reward if we believe it, and a threat of dire punishment if we do not, the Self-appointed Superior Class has driven men wheresoever it willed. The evolution of formal religions is not a complex process, and the fact that they embody these two unmixable things, dogma and morality, is a very plain and simple truth, easily seen, undisputed by all reasonable men. And be it said that the morality of most religions is good. Love, truth, charity, justice and gentleness are taught in them all. But, like a rule in Greek grammar, there are many exceptions. And so in the morality of religions there are exceptional instances that constantly arise where love, truth, charity, gentleness and justice are waived on suggestion of the Superior Class, that good may follow. Were it not for these exceptions there would be no wars between Christian nations.

The question of how to express your life will probably never down, for the reason that men vary in temperament and inclination. Some men have no capacity for certain sins of the flesh; others there be, who, having lost their inclination for sensuality through too much indulgence, turn ascetics. Yet all sermons have but one theme: how shall life be expressed? Between asceticism and indulgence men and races swing.

Asceticism in our day finds an interesting manifestation in the Trappists, who live on a mountain top, nearly inaccessible, and deprive themselves of almost every vestige of bodily comfort, going without food for days, wearing uncomfortable garments, suffering severe cold; and should one of this community look upon the face of a woman he would think he was in instant danger of damnation. So here we find the extreme instance of men repressing the faculties of the body in order that the spirit may find ample time and opportunity for exercise.

Somewhere between this extreme repression of the monk and the license of the sensualist lies the truth. But just where is the great question; and the desire of one person, who thinks he has discovered the norm, to compel all other men to stop there, has led to war and strife untold. All law centers around this point—what shall men be allowed to do? And so we find statutes to punish "strolling play actors," "players on fiddles," "disturbers of the public conscience," "persons who dance wantonly," "blasphemers," and in England there were, in the year 1800, thirty-seven offenses that were legally punishable by death. What expression is right and what is not, is simply a matter of opinion. One religious denomination that now exists does not allow singing; instrumental music has been to some a rock of offense, exciting the spirit through the sense of hearing, to improper thoughts—"through the lascivious pleasing of the lute"; others think dancing wicked, while a few allow pipe-organ music, but draw the line at the violin; while still others use a whole orchestra in their religious service. Some there be who regard pictures as implements of idolatry; while the Hook-and-Eye Baptists look upon buttons as immoral.

Strange evolutions are often witnessed within the life of one individual. For instance, Leo Tolstoy, a great and good man, at one time a sensualist, has now turned ascetic; a common evolution in the lives of the saints. But excellent as this man is, there is yet a grave imperfection in his cosmos which to a degree vitiates the truth he desires to teach: he leaves the element of beauty out of his formula. Not caring for harmony as set forth in color, form and sweet sounds, he is quite willing to deny all others these things which minister to their well-being. There is in most souls a hunger for beauty, just as there is physical hunger. Beauty speaks to their spirits through the senses; but Tolstoy would have your house barren to the verge of hardship. My veneration for Count Tolstoy is profound, yet I mention him here to show the grave danger that lies in allowing any man, even one of the wisest of men, to dictate to us what is best. We ourselves are the better judges. Most of the frightful cruelties inflicted on men during the past have arisen simply out of a difference of opinion that arose through a difference in temperament. The question is as alive to-day as it was two thousand years ago—what expression is best? That is, what shall we do to be saved? And concrete absurdity consists in saying that we must all do the same thing. Whether the race will ever grow to a point where men will be willing to leave the matter of life-expression to the individual is a question; but the millennium will never arrive until men cease trying to compel all other men to live after one pattern.

Most people are anxious to do what is best for themselves and least harmful for others. The average man now has intelligence enough: Utopia is not far off, if the self-appointed folk who rule us, and teach us for a consideration, would only be willing to do unto others as they would be done by, that is to say, mind their own business and cease coveting things that belong to other people. War among nations and strife among individuals is a result of the covetous spirit to possess.

A little more patience, a little more charity for all, a little more love; with less bowing down to the past, and the silent ignoring of pretended authority; a brave looking forward to the future, with more self-confidence and more faith in our fellow men, and the race will be ripe for a great burst of life and light.

Time and Chance

As the subject is somewhat complex, I will have to explain it to you. The first point is that there is not so very much difference in the intelligence of people after all. The great man is not so great as folks think, and the dull man is not quite so stupid as he seems. The difference in our estimates of men lies in the fact that one individual is able to get his goods into the show-window, and the other is not aware that he has any show-window or any goods.

"The soul knows all things, and knowledge is only a remembering," says Emerson.

This seems a very broad statement; and yet the fact remains that the vast majority of men know a thousand times as much as they are aware of. Far down in the silent depths of subconsciousness lie myriads of truths, each awaiting a time when its owner shall call it forth. To utilize these stored-up thoughts, you must express them to others; and to be able to express them well your soul has to soar into this subconscious realm where you have cached these net results of experience. In other words, you must "come out"—get out of self—away from self-consciousness, into the region of partial oblivion—away from the boundaries of time and the limitations of space. The great painter forgets all in the presence of his canvas; the writer is oblivious to his surroundings; the singer floats away on the wings of melody (and carries the audience with her); the orator pours out his soul for an hour, and it seems to him as if barely five minutes had passed, so rapt is he in his exalted theme. When you reach the heights of sublimity and are expressing your highest and best, you are in a partial trance condition. And all men who enter this condition surprise themselves by the quantity of knowledge and the extent of insight they possess. And some going a little deeper than others into this trance condition, and having no knowledge of the miraculous storing up of truth in the subconscious cells, jump to the conclusion that their intelligence is guided by a spirit not theirs. When one reaches this conclusion he begins to wither at the top, for he relies on the dead, and ceases to feed the well-springs of his subconscious self.

The mind is a dual affair—objective and subjective. The objective mind sees all, hears all, reasons things out. The subjective mind stores up and only gives out when the objective mind sleeps. And as few men ever cultivate the absorbed, reflective or semi-trance state, where the objective mind rests, they never really call on their subconscious treasury for its stores. They are always self-conscious.

A man in commerce, where men prey on their kind, must be alive and alert to what is going on, or while he dreams, his competitor will seize upon his birthright. And so you see why poets are poor and artists often beg.

And the summing up of this sermonette is that all men are equally rich, only some thru fate are able to muster their mental legions on the plains of their being and count them, while others are never able to do so.

But what think you is necessary before a person can come into full possession of his subconscious treasures? Well, I'll tell you: It is not ease, nor prosperity, nor requited love, nor worldly security—not these.

"You sing well," said the master, impatiently, to his best pupil, "but you will never sing divinely until you have given your all for love, and then been neglected and rejected, and scorned and beaten, and left for dead. Then, if you do not exactly die, you will come back, and when the world hears your voice it will mistake you for an angel and fall at your feet."

And the moral is, that as long as you are satisfied and comfortable, you use only the objective mind and live in the world of sense. But let love be torn from your grasp and flee as a shadow—living only as a memory in a haunting sense of loss; let death come and the sky shut down over less worth in the world; or stupid misunderstanding and crushing defeat grind you into the dust, then you may arise, forgetting time and space and self, and take refuge in mansions not made with hands; and find a certain sad, sweet satisfaction in the contemplation of treasures stored up where moth and rust do not corrupt, and where thieves do not break through and steal.

And thus looking out into the Eternal, you entirely forget the present and go forth into the Land of Subconsciousness—the Land of Spirit, where yet dwell the gods of ancient and innocent days? Is it worth the cost?

Psychology of a Religious Revival

Traveling to and fro over the land and up and down in it are men who manage street-fairs.

Let it be known that a street-fair or Mardi Gras is never a spontaneous expression of the carnival spirit on the part of the townspeople. These festivals are a business—carefully planned, well advertised and carried out with much astuteness.

The men who manage street-fairs send advance agents, to make arrangements with the local merchants of the place—these secure the legal permits that are necessary.

A week is set apart for the carnival, much advertising is done, the newspapers, reflecting the will of the many, devote pages to the wonderful things that will happen. The shows arrive—the touters, the spielers, the clowns, the tumblers, the girls in tights, the singers! The bands play—the carnival is on! The object of the fair is to boom the business of the town. The object of the professional managers of the fair is to make money for themselves, and this they do thru the guaranty of the merchants, or a percentage on concessions, or both.

I am told that no town whose business is on an absolutely safe and secure footing ever resorts to a street-fair. The street-fair comes in when a rival town seems to be getting more than its share of the trade. When the business of Skaneateles is drifting to Waterloo, then Skaneateles succumbs to a street-fair.

Sanitation, sewerage, good water supply, and school-houses and paved streets are not the result of throwing confetti, tooting tin horns and waiving the curfew law.

Whether commerce is effectually helped by the street-fair, or a town assisted to get on a firm financial basis through the ministry of the tom-tom, is a problem. I leave the question with students of political economy and pass on to a local condition which is not a theory. The religious revivals that have recently been conducted in various parts of the country were most carefully planned business schemes. One F. Wilbur Chapman and his corps of well-trained associates may be taken as a type of the individuals who work up local religious excitement for a consideration.

Religious revivals are managed very much as are street-fairs. If religion is getting at a low ebb in your town, you can hire Chapman, the revivalist, just as you can secure the services of Farley, the strike-breaker. Chapman and his helpers go from town to town and from city to city and work up this excitation as a business. They are paid for their services a thousand dollars a week, or down to what they can get from collections. Sometimes they work on a guaranty, and at other times on a percentage or contingent fee, or both.

Towns especially in need of Mr. Chapman's assistance will please send for circulars, terms and testimonials. No souls saved—no pay.

The basic element of the revival is hypnotism. The scheme of bringing about the hypnosis, or the obfuscation of the intellect, has taken generations to carefully perfect. The plan is first to depress the spirit to a point where the subject is incapable of independent thought. Mournful music, a monotonous voice of woe, tearful appeals to God, dreary groans, the whole mingled with pious ejaculations, all tend to produce a terrifying effect upon the auditor. The thought of God's displeasure is constantly dwelt upon—the idea of guilt, death and eternal torment. If the victims can be made to indulge in hysterical laughter occasionally, the control is better brought about. No chance is allowed for repose, poise or sane consideration. When the time seems ripe a general promise of joy is made and the music takes an adagio turn. The speaker's voice now tells of triumph—offers of forgiveness are tendered, and then the promise of eternal life.

The final intent is to get the victim on his feet and make him come forward and acknowledge the fetich. This once done the convert finds himself among pleasant companions. His social station is improved—people shake hands with him and solicitously ask after his welfare. His approbativeness is appealed to—his position is now one of importance. And moreover, he is given to understand in many subtle ways that as he will be damned in another world if he does not acquiesce in the fetich, so also will he be damned financially and socially here if he does not join the church. The intent in every Christian community is to boycott and make a social outcast of the independent thinker. The fetich furnishes excuse for the hypnotic processes. Without assuming a personal God who can be appeased, eternal damnation and the proposition that you can win eternal life by believing a myth, there is no sane reason for the absurd hypnotic formulas.

We are heirs to the past, its good and ill, and we all have a touch of superstition, like a syphilitic taint. To eradicate this tyranny of fear and get the cringe and crawl out of our natures, seems the one desirable thing to lofty minds. But the revivalist, knowing human nature, as all confidence men do, banks on our superstitious fears and makes his appeal to our acquisitiveness, offering us absolution and life eternal for a consideration—to cover expenses. As long as men are paid honors and money, can wear good clothes, and be immune from work for preaching superstition, they will preach it. The hope of the world lies in withholding supplies from the pious mendicants who seek to hold our minds in thrall.

This idea of a divine bankrupt court where you can get forgiveness by paying ten cents on the dollar, with the guaranty of becoming a winged pauper of the skies, is not alluring excepting to a man who has been well scared. Advance agents pave the way for revivalists by arranging details with the local orthodox clergy. Universalists, Unitarians, Christian Scientists and Befaymillites are all studiously avoided. The object is to fill depleted pews of orthodox Protestant churches—these pay the freight, and to the victor belong the spoils. The plot and plan is to stampede into the pen of orthodoxy the intellectual unwary—children and neurotic grown-ups. The cap-and-bells element is largely represented in Chapman's select company of German-American talent: the confetti of foolishness is thrown at us—we dodge, laugh, listen and no one has time to think, weigh, sift or analyze. There are the boom of rhetoric, the crack of confession, the interspersed rebel-yell of triumph, the groans of despair, the cries of victory.

Then come songs by paid singers, the pealing of the organ—rise and sing, kneel and pray, entreaty, condemnation, misery, tears, threats, promise, joy, happiness, heaven, eternal bliss, decide now—not a moment is to be lost, whoop-la you'll be a long time in hell!

All this whirl is a carefully prepared plan, worked out by expert flim-flammers to addle the reason, scramble intellect and make of men drooling derelicts.

What for?

I'll tell you—that Doctor Chapman and his professional rooters may roll in cheap honors, be immune from all useful labor and wax fat on the pay of those who work. Second, that the orthodox churches may not advance into workshops and schoolhouses, but may remain forever the home of a superstition. One would think that the promise of making a person exempt from the results of his own misdeeds, would turn the man of brains from these religious shell-men in disgust. But under their hypnotic spell, the minds of many seem to suffer an obsession, and they are caught in the swirl of foolish feeling, like a grocer's clerk in the hands of a mesmerist.

At Northfield, Massachusetts, is a college at which men are taught and trained, just as men are drilled at a Tonsorial College, in every phase of this pleasing episcopopography.

There is a good fellow by the suggestive name of Sunday who works the religious graft. Sunday is the whirling dervish up to date. He and Chapman and their cappers purposely avoid any trace of the ecclesiastic in their attire. They dress like drummers—trousers carefully creased, two watch-chains and a warm vest. Their manner is free and easy, their attitude familiar. The way they address the Almighty reveals that their reverence for Him springs out of the supposition that He is very much like themselves.

The indelicacy of the revivalists who recently called meetings to pray for Fay Mills, was shown in their ardent supplications to God that He should make Mills to be like them. Fay Mills tells of the best way to use this life here and now. He does not prophesy what will become of you if you do not accept his belief, neither does he promise everlasting life as a reward for thinking as he does. He realizes that he has not the agency of everlasting life. Fay Mills is more interested in having a soul that is worth saving than in saving a soul that isn't. Chapman talks about lost souls as he might about collar buttons lost under a bureau, just as if God ever misplaced anything, or that all souls were not God's souls, and therefore forever in His keeping.

Doctor Chapman wants all men to act alike and believe alike, not realizing that progress is the result of individuality, and so long as a man thinks, whether he is right or wrong, he is making head. Neither does he realize that wrong thinking is better than no thinking at all, and that the only damnation consists in ceasing to think, and accepting the conclusions of another. Final truths and final conclusions are wholly unthinkable to sensible people in their sane moments, but these revivalists wish to sum up truth for all time and put their leaden seal upon it.

In Los Angeles is a preacher by the name of McIntyre, a type of the blatant Bellarmine who exiled Galileo—a man who never doubts his own infallibility, who talks like an oracle and continually tells of perdition for all who disagree with him.

Needless to say that McIntyre lacks humor. Personally, I prefer the McGregors, but in Los Angeles the

McIntyres are popular. It was McIntyre who called a meeting to pray for Fay Mills, and in proposing the meeting McIntyre made the unblushing announcement that he had never met Mills nor heard him speak, nor had he read one of his books.

Chapman and McIntyre represent the modern types of Phariseeism—spielers and spouters for churchianity, and such are the men who make superstition of so long life. Superstition is the one Infamy—Voltaire was right. To pretend to believe a thing at which your reason revolts—to stultify your intellect—this, if it exists at all, is the unpardonable sin. These muftis preach "the blood of Jesus," the dogma that man without a belief in miracles is eternally lost, that everlasting life depends upon acknowledging this, that or the other. Self-reliance, self-control and self-respect are the three things that make a man a man.

But man has so recently taken on this ability to think, that he has not yet gotten used to handling it. The tool is cumbrous in his hands. He is afraid of it—this one characteristic that differentiates him from the lower animals—so he abdicates and turns his divine birthright over to a syndicate. This combination called a church agrees to take care of his doubts and fears and do his thinking for him, and to help matters along he is assured that he is not fit to think for himself, and to do so would be a sin. Man, in his present crude state, holds somewhat the same attitude toward reason that an Apache Indian holds toward a camera—the Indian thinks that to have his picture taken means that he will shrivel up and blow away in a month. And Stanley relates that a watch with its constant ticking sent the bravest of Congo chiefs into a cold sweat of agonizing fear; on discovering which, the explorer had but to draw his Waterbury and threaten to turn the whole bunch into crocodiles, and at once they got busy and did his bidding. Stanley exhibited the true Northfield-revival quality in banking on the superstition of his wavering and frightened followers.

The revival meetin' is an orgie of the soul, a spiritual debauch—a dropping from sane and sensible control into eroticism. No person of normal intelligence can afford to throw the reins of reason on the neck of emotion and ride a Tam O'Shanter race to Bedlam. This hysteria of the uncurbed feelings is the only blasphemy, and if there were a personal God, He surely would be grieved to see that we have so absurd an idea of Him, as to imagine He would be pleased with our deporting the divine gift of reason into the hell-box.

Revivalism works up the voltage, then makes no use of the current—the wire is grounded. Let any one of these revivalists write out his sermons and print them in a book, and no sane man could read them without danger of paresis. The book would lack synthesis, defy analysis, puzzle the brain and paralyze the will. There would not be enough attic salt in it to save it. It would be the supernaculum of the commonplace, and prove the author to be the lobscouse of literature, the loblolly of letters. The churches want to enroll members, and so desperate is the situation that they are willing to get them at the price of self-respect. Hence come Sunday, Monday, Tuesday and Chapman, and play Svengali to our Trilby. These gentlemen use the methods and the tricks of the auctioneer—the blandishments of the bookmaker—the sleek, smooth ways of the professional spieler.

With this troupe of Christian clowns is one Chaeffer, who is a specialist with children. He has meetings for boys and girls only, where he plays tricks, grimaces, tells stories and gets his little hearers laughing, and thus having found an entrance into their hearts, he suddenly reverses the lever, and has them crying. He talks to these little innocents about sin, the wrath of God, the death of Christ, and offers them a choice between everlasting life and eternal death. To the person who knows and loves children—who has studied the gentle ways of Froebel—this excitement is vicious, concrete cruelty. Weakened vitality follows close upon overwrought nerves, and every excess has its penalty—the pendulum swings as far this way as it does that.

These reverend gentlemen bray it into the ears of innocent little children that they were born in iniquity, and in sin did their mothers conceive them; that the souls of all children over nine years (why nine?) are lost, and the only way they can hope for heaven is through a belief in a barbaric blood bamboozle, that men of intelligence have long since discarded. And all this in the name of the gentle Christ, who took little children in his arms and said, "Of such is the Kingdom of Heaven."

This pagan proposition of being born in sin is pollution to the mind of a child, and causes misery, unrest and heartache incomputable. A few years ago we were congratulating ourselves that the devil at last was dead, and that the tears of pity had put out the fires of hell, but the serpent of superstition was only slightly scotched, not killed.

The intent of the religious revival is dual: first, the claim is that conversion makes men lead better lives; second, it saves their souls from endless death or everlasting hell.

To make men lead beautiful lives is excellent, but the Reverend Doctor Chapman, nor any of his colleagues, nor the denominations that they represent, will for an instant admit that the fact of a man living a beautiful life will save his soul alive In fact, Doctor Chapman,

Doctor Torrey and Doctor Sunday, backed by the Reverend Doctor McIntyre, repeatedly warn their hearers of the danger of a morality that is not accompanied by a belief in the "blood of Jesus."

So the beautiful life they talk of is the bait that covers the hook for gudgeons. You have to accept the superstition, or your beautiful life to them is a byword and a hissing.

Hence, to them, superstition, and not conduct, is the vital thing.

If such a belief is not fanaticism then have I read Webster's Unabridged Dictionary in vain. Belief in superstition makes no man kinder, gentler, more useful to himself or society. He can have all the virtues without the fetich, and he may have the fetich and all the vices beside. Morality is really not controlled at all by religion—if statistics of reform schools and prisons are to be believed.

Fay Mills, according to Reverend Doctor McIntyre has all the virtues—he is forgiving, kind, gentle, modest, helpful. But Fay has abandoned the fetich—hence McIntyre and Chapman call upon the public to pray for Fay Mills. Mills had the virtues when he believed in the fetich—and now that he has disavowed the fetich, he still has the virtues, and in a degree he never before had. Even those who oppose him admit this, but still they declare that he is forever "lost."

Reverend Doctor Chaeffer says there are two kinds of habits—good and bad.

There are also two kinds of religion, good and bad. The religion of kindness, good cheer, helpfulness and useful effort is good. And on this point there is no dispute—it is admitted everywhere by every grade of intellect. But any form of religion that incorporates a belief in miracles and other barbaric superstitions, as a necessity to salvation, is not only bad, but very bad. And all men, if left alone long enough to think, know that salvation depends upon redemption from a belief in miracles. But the intent of Doctor Chapman and his theological rough riders is to stampede the herd and set it a milling. To rope the mavericks and place upon them the McIntyre brand is then quite easy.

As for the reaction and the cleaning up after the carnival, our revivalists are not concerned. The confetti, collapsed balloons and peanut shucks are the net assets of the revival—and these are left for the local managers.

Revivals are for the revivalists, and some fine morning these revival towns will arise, rub their sleepy eyes, and Chapman will be but a bad taste in the mouth, and Sunday, Chaeffer, Torrey, Biederwolf and Company, a troubled dream. To preach hagiology to civilized people is a lapse that Nemesis will not overlook. America stands for the Twentieth Century, and if in a moment of weakness she slips back to the exuberant folly of the frenzied piety of the Sixteenth, she must pay the penalty. Two things man will have to do—get free from the bondage of other men; and second, liberate himself from the phantoms of his own mind. On neither of these points does the revivalist help or aid in any way. Effervescence is not character and every debauch must be paid for in vitality and self-respect.

All formal organized religions through which the promoters and managers thrive are bad, but some are worse than others. The more superstition a religion has, the worse it is. Usually religions are made up of morality and superstition. Pure superstition alone would be revolting—in our day it would attract nobody—so the idea is introduced that morality and religion are inseparable. I am against the men who pretend to believe that ethics without a fetich is vain and useless.

The preachers who preach the beauty of truth, honesty and a useful, helpful life, I am with, head, heart and hand.

The preachers who declare that there can be no such thing as a beautiful life unless it will accept superstition, I am against, tooth, claw, club, tongue and pen. Down with the Infamy! I prophesy a day when business and education will be synonymous—when commerce and college will join hands—when the preparation for life will be to go to work.

As long as trade was trickery, business barter, commerce finesse, government exploitation, slaughter honorable, and murder a fine art; when religion was ignorant superstition, piety the worship of a fetich and education a clutch for honors, there was small hope for the race. Under these conditions everything tended towards division, dissipation, disintegration, separation—darkness, death.

But with the supremacy gained by science, the introduction of the one-price system in business, and the gradually growing conviction that honesty is man's most valuable asset, we behold light at the end of the tunnel.

It only remains now for the laity to drive conviction home upon the clergy, and prove to them that pretence has its penalty, and to bring to the mourners' bench that trinity of offenders, somewhat ironically designated as the Three Learned Professions, and mankind will be well out upon the broad highway, the towering domes of the Ideal City in sight.

ONE-MAN POWER

Every successful concern is the result of a One-Man Power. Cooeperation, technically, is an iridescent dream—things cooeperate because the man makes them. He cements them by his will.

But find this Man, and get his confidence, and his weary eyes will look into yours and the cry of his heart shall echo in your ears. "O, for some one to help me bear this burden!"

Then he will tell you of his endless search for Ability, and of his continual disappointments and thwartings in trying to get some one to help himself by helping him.

Ability is the one crying need of the hour. The banks are bulging with money, and everywhere are men looking for work. The harvest is ripe. But the Ability to captain the unemployed and utilize the capital, is lacking—sadly lacking. In every city there are many five-and ten-thousand-dollar-a-year positions to be filled, but the only applicants are men who want jobs at fifteen dollars a week. Your man of Ability has a place already. Yes, Ability is a rare article.

But there is something that is much scarcer, something finer far, something rarer than this quality of Ability.

It is the ability to recognize Ability.

The sternest comment that ever can be made against employers as a class, lies in the fact that men of Ability usually succeed in showing their worth in spite of their employer, and not with his assistance and encouragement.

If you know the lives of men of Ability, you know that they discovered their power, almost without exception, thru chance or accident. Had the accident not occurred that made the opportunity, the man would have remained unknown and practically lost to the world. The experience of Tom Potter, telegraph operator at an obscure little way station, is truth painted large. That fearful night, when most of the wires were down and a passenger train went through the bridge, gave Tom Potter the opportunity of discovering himself. He took charge of the dead, cared for the wounded, settled fifty claims—drawing drafts on the company—burned the last vestige of the wreck, sunk the waste iron in the river and repaired the bridge before the arrival of the Superintendent on the spot.

"Who gave you the authority to do all this?" demanded the Superintendent.

"Nobody," replied Tom, "I assumed the authority."

The next month Tom Potter's salary was five thousand dollars a year, and in three years he was making ten times this, simply because he could get other men to do things.

Why wait for an accident to discover Tom Potter? Let us set traps for Tom Potter, and lie in wait for him. Perhaps Tom Potter is just around the corner, across the street, in the next room, or at our elbow. Myriads of embryonic Tom Potters await discovery and development if we but look for them.

I know a man who roamed the woods and fields for thirty years and never found an Indian arrow. One day he began to think "arrow," and stepping out of his doorway he picked one up. Since then he has collected a bushel of them.

Suppose we cease wailing about incompetence, sleepy indifference and slipshod "help" that watches the clock. These things exist—let us dispose of the subject by admitting it, and then emphasize the fact that freckled farmer boys come out of the West and East and often go to the front and do things in a masterly way. There is one name that stands out in history like a beacon light after all these twenty-five hundred years have passed, just because the man had the sublime genius of discovering Ability. That man is Pericles. Pericles made Athens.

And to-day the very dust of the streets of Athens is being sifted and searched for relics and remnants of the things made by people who were captained by men of Ability who were discovered by Pericles.

There is very little competition in this line of discovering Ability. We sit down and wail because Ability does not come our way. Let us think "Ability," and possibly we can jostle Pericles there on his pedestal, where he has stood for over a score of centuries—the man with a supreme genius for recognizing Ability. Hail to thee, Pericles, and hail to thee, Great Unknown, who shall be the first to successfully imitate this captain of men.

Mental Attitude

Success is in the blood. There are men whom fate can never keep down—they march forward in a jaunty manner, and take by divine right the best of everything that the earth affords. But their success is not attained by means of the Samuel Smiles-Connecticut policy. They do not lie in wait, nor scheme, nor fawn, nor seek to adapt their sails to catch the breeze of popular favor. Still, they are ever alert and alive to any good that may come their way, and when it comes they simply appropriate it, and tarrying not, move steadily on.

Good health! Whenever you go out of doors, draw the chin in, carry the crown of the head high, and fill the lungs to the utmost; drink in the sunshine; greet your friends with a smile, and put soul into every hand-clasp.

Do not fear being misunderstood; and never waste a moment thinking about your enemies. Try to fix firmly in your own mind what you would like to do, and then without violence of direction you will move straight to the goal.

Fear is the rock on which we split, and hate the shoal on which many a barque is stranded. When we become fearful, the judgment is as unreliable as the compass of a ship whose hold is full of iron ore; when we hate, we have unshipped the rudder; and if ever we stop to meditate on what the gossips say, we have allowed a hawser to foul the screw.

Keep your mind on the great and splendid thing you would like to do; and then, as the days go gliding by, you will find yourself unconsciously seizing the opportunities that are required for the fulfillment of your desire, just as the coral insect takes from the running tide the elements that it needs. Picture in your mind the able, earnest, useful person you desire to be, and the thought that you hold is hourly transforming you into that particular individual you so admire.

Thought is supreme, and to think is often better than to do.

Preserve a right mental attitude—the attitude of courage, frankness and good cheer.

Darwin and Spencer have told us that this is the method of Creation. Each animal has evolved the parts it needed and desired. The horse is fleet because he wishes to be; the bird flies because it desires to; the duck has a web foot because it wants to swim. All things come through desire and every sincere prayer is answered. We become like that on which our hearts are fixed.

Many people know this, but they do not know it thoroughly enough so that it shapes their lives. We want friends, so we scheme and chase 'cross lots after strong people, and lie in wait for good folks—or alleged good folks—hoping to be able to attach ourselves to them. The only way to secure friends is to be one. And before you are fit for friendship you must be able to do without it. That is to say, you must have sufficient self-reliance to take care of yourself, and then out of the surplus of your energy you can do for others.

The individual who craves friendship, and yet desires a self-centered spirit more, will never lack for friends.

If you would have friends, cultivate solitude instead of society. Drink in the ozone; bathe in the sunshine; and out in the silent night, under the stars, say to yourself again and yet again, "I am a part of all my eyes behold!" And the feeling then will come to you that you are no mere interloper between earth and heaven; but you are a necessary part of the whole. No harm can come to you that does not come to all, and if you shall go down it can only be amid a wreck of worlds.

Like old Job, that which we fear will surely come upon us. By a wrong mental attitude we have set in motion a train of events that ends in disaster. People who die in middle life from disease, almost without exception, are those who have been preparing for death. The acute tragic condition is simply the result of a chronic state of mind—a culmination of a series of events.

Character is the result of two things, mental attitude, and the way we spend our time. It is what we think and what we do that make us what we are.

By laying hold on the forces of the universe, you are strong with them. And when you realize this, all else is easy, for in your arteries will course red corpuscles, and in your heart the determined resolution is born to do and to be. Carry your chin in and the crown of your head high. We are gods in the chrysalis.

The Outsider

WHEN I was a farmer lad I noticed that whenever we bought a new cow, and turned her into the pasture with the herd, there was a general inclination on the part of the rest to make the new cow think she had landed in the orthodox perdition. They would hook her away from the salt, chase her from the water, and the long-horned ones, for several weeks, would lose no opportunity to give her vigorous digs, pokes and prods.

With horses it was the same. And I remember one particular little black mare that we boys used to transfer from one pasture to another, just to see her back into a herd of horses and hear her hoofs play a resounding solo on their ribs as they gathered round to do her mischief.

Men are animals just as much as are cows, horses and pigs; and they manifest similar proclivities. The introduction of a new man into an institution always causes a small panic of resentment, especially if he be a person of some power. Even in schools and colleges the new teacher has to fight his way to overcome the opposition he is certain to meet.

In a lumber camp, the newcomer would do well to take the initiative, like that little black mare, and meet the first black look with a short-arm jab.

But in a bank, department store or railroad office this cannot be. So the next best thing is to endure, and win out by an attention to business to which the place is unaccustomed. In any event, the bigger the man, unless he has the absolute power to overawe everything, the more uncomfortable will be his position until gradually time smooths the way and new issues come up for criticism, opposition and resentment, and he is forgotten.

The idea of Civil Service Reform—promotion for the good men in your employ rather than hiring new ones for the big places—is a rule which looks well on paper but is a fatal policy if carried out to the letter.

The business that is not progressive is sowing the seeds of its own dissolution. Life is a movement forward, and all things in nature that are not evolving into something better are preparing to return into their constituent elements. One general rule for progress in big business concerns is the introduction of new blood. You must keep step with the business world. If you lag behind, the outlaws that hang on the flanks of commerce will cut you out and take you captive, just as the wolves lie in wait for the sick cow of the plains.

To keep your columns marching you must introduce new methods, new inspiration and seize upon the best that others have invented or discovered.

The great railroads of America have evolved together. No one of them has an appliance or a method that is much beyond the rest. If it were not for this interchange of men and ideas some railroads would still be using the link and pin, and snake-heads would be as common as in the year 1869.

The railroad manager who knows his business is ever on the lookout for excellence among his men, and he promotes those who give an undivided service. But besides this he hires a strong man occasionally from the outside and promotes him over everybody. Then out come the hammers!

But this makes but little difference to your competent manager—if a place is to be filled and he has no one on his payroll big enough to fill it, he hires an outsider.

That is right and well for every one concerned. The new life of many a firm dates from the day they hired a new man.

Communities that intermarry raise a fine crop of scrubs, and the result is the same in business ventures. Two of America's largest publishing houses failed for a tidy sum of five millions or so each, a few years ago, just thru a dogged policy, that extended over a period of fifty years, of promoting cousins, uncles and aunts whose only claim of efficiency was that they had been on the pension roll for a long time. This way lies dry-rot.

If you are a business man, and have a position of responsibility to be filled, look carefully among your old helpers for a man to promote. But if you haven't a man big enough to fill the place, do not put in a little one for the sake of peace. Go outside and find a man and hire him—never mind the salary if he can man the position—wages are always relative to earning power. This will be the only way you can really man your ship.

As for Civil Service Rules—rules are made to be broken. And as for the long-horned ones who will attempt to make life miserable for your new employe, be patient with them. It is the privilege of everybody to do a reasonable amount of kicking, especially if the person has been a long time with one concern and has received many benefits.

But if at the last, worst comes to worst, do not forget that you yourself are at the head of the concern. If it fails you get the blame. And should the anvil chorus become so persistent that there is danger of discord taking the place of harmony, stand by your new man, even tho it is necessary to give the blue envelope to every antediluvian. Precedence in business is a matter of power, and years in one position may mean that the man has been there so long that he needs a change. Let the zephyrs of natural law play freely thru your whiskers.

So here is the argument: promote your deserving men, but do not be afraid to hire a keen outsider; he helps everybody, even the kickers, for if you disintegrate and go down in defeat, the kickers will have to skirmish around for new jobs anyway. Isn't that so?

GET OUT OR GET IN LINE

A BRAHAM LINCOLN'S letter to Hooker! If all the letters, messages and speeches of Lincoln were destroyed, except that one letter to Hooker, we still would have an excellent index to the heart of the Rail-Splitter.

In this letter we see that Lincoln ruled his own spirit; and we also behold the fact that he could rule others. The letter shows wise diplomacy, frankness, kindliness, wit, tact and infinite patience. Hooker had harshly and unjustly criticised Lincoln, his commander in chief. But Lincoln waives all this in deference to the virtues he believes Hooker possesses, and promotes him to succeed Burnside. In other words, the man who had been wronged promotes the man who had wronged him, over the head of a man whom the promotee had wronged and for whom the promoter had a warm personal friendship.

But all personal considerations were sunk in view of the end desired. Yet it was necessary that the man promoted should know the truth, and Lincoln told it to him in a way that did not humiliate nor fire to foolish anger; but which surely prevented the attack of cerebral elephantiasis to which Hooker was liable.

Perhaps we had better give the letter entire, and so here it is:

> Executive Mansion,
> Washington, January 26, 1863.
>
> *Major-General Hooker:*
>
> *General:*—I have placed you at the head of the Army of the Potomac. Of course, I have done this upon what appear to me to be sufficient reasons, and yet I think it best for you to know that there are some things in regard to which I am not quite satisfied with you.
>
> I believe you to be a brave and skilful soldier, which, of course, I like. I also believe you do not mix politics with your position, in which you are right.
>
> You have confidence in yourself, which is a valuable if not an indispensable quality.
>
> You are ambitious, which, within reasonable bounds, does good rather than harm; but I think that during General Burnside's command of the army you have taken counsel of your ambition and thwarted him as much as you could, in which you did a great wrong to the country, and to a most meritorious and honorable brother officer.
>
> I have heard, in such a way as to believe it, of your recently saying that both the army and the government needed a dictator. Of course, it was not for this, but in spite of it, that I have given you the command. Only those generals who gain successes can set up dictators. What I now ask of you is military success, and I will risk the dictatorship. The government will support you to the utmost of its abil-

ity, which is neither more nor less than it has done and will do for all commanders. I much fear that the spirit you have aided to infuse into the army, of criticising their commander and withholding confidence from him, will now turn upon you. I shall assist you as far as I can to put it down. Neither you nor Napoleon, if he were alive again, could get any good out of an army while such a spirit prevails in it. And now beware of rashness, but with sleepless vigilance go forward and give us victories.

Yours very truly,
A. LINCOLN.

One point in this letter is especially worth our consideration, for it suggests a condition that springs up like deadly nightshade from a poisonous soil. I refer to the habit of carping, sneering, grumbling and criticising those who are above us. The man who is anybody and who does anything is certainly going to be criticised, vilified and misunderstood. This is a part of the penalty for greatness, and every great man understands it; and understands, too, that it is no proof of greatness. The final proof of greatness lies in being able to endure contumely without resentment. Lincoln did not resent criticism; he knew that every life was its own excuse for being, but look how he calls Hooker's attention to the fact that the dissension Hooker has sown is going to return and plague him! "Neither you, nor Napoleon, if he were alive, could get any good out of an army while such a spirit prevails in it." Hooker's fault falls on Hooker—others suffer, but Hooker suffers most of all.

Not long ago I met a Yale student home on a vacation. I am sure he did not represent the true Yale spirit, for he was full of criticism and bitterness toward the institution. President Hadley came in for his share, and I was given items, facts, data, with times and places, for a "peach of a roast."

Very soon I saw the trouble was not with Yale, the trouble was with the young man. He had mentally dwelt on some trivial slights until he had gotten so out of harmony with the place that he had lost the power to derive any benefit from it. Yale college is not a perfect institution—a fact, I suppose, that President Hadley and most Yale men are quite willing to admit; but Yale does supply young men certain advantages, and it depends upon the students whether they will avail themselves of these advantages or not. If you are a student in college, seize upon the good that is there. You receive good by giving it. You gain by giving—so give sympathy and cheerful loyalty to the institution. Be proud of it. Stand by your teachers—they are doing the best they can. If the place is faulty, make it a better place by an example of cheerfully doing your work every day the best you can. Mind your own business.

If the concern where you are employed is all wrong, and the Old Man is a curmudgeon, it may be well for you to go to the Old Man and confidentially, quietly and kindly tell him that his policy is absurd and preposterous. Then show him how to reform his ways, and you might offer to take charge of the concern and cleanse it of its secret faults. Do this, or if for any reason you should prefer not, then take your choice of these: Get Out, or Get in Line. You have got to do one or the other—now make your choice. If you work for a man, in heaven's name work for him.

If he pays you wages that supply you your bread and butter, work for him—speak well of him, think well of him, stand by him and stand by the institution that he represents.

I think if I worked for a man, I would work for him. I would not work for him a part of the time, and the rest of the time work against him. I would give an undivided service or none. If put to the pinch, an ounce of loyalty is worth a pound of cleverness.

If you must vilify, condemn and eternally disparage, why, resign your position, and then when you are outside, damn to your heart's content. But I pray you, as long as you are a part of an institution, do not condemn it. Not that you will injure the institution—not that—but when you disparage a concern of which you are a part, you disparage yourself.

More than that, you are loosening the tendrils that hold you to the institution, and the first high wind that happens along, you will be uprooted and blown away in the blizzard's track—and probably you will never know why. The letter only says, "Times are dull and we regret there is not enough work," et cetera.

Everywhere you will find these out-of-a-job fellows. Talk with them and you will find that they are full of railing, bitterness, scorn and condemnation. That was the trouble—thru a spirit of fault-finding they got themselves swung around so they blocked the channel, and had to be dynamited. They were out of harmony with the place, and no longer being a help they had to be removed. Every employer is constantly looking for people who can help him; naturally he is on the lookout among his employees for those who do not help, and everything and everybody that is a hindrance has to go. This is the law of trade—do not find fault with it; it is founded on nature. The reward is only for the man who helps, and in order to help you must have sympathy.

You cannot help the Old Man so long as you are explaining in an undertone and whisper, by gesture and suggestion, by thought and mental attitude that he is a curmudgeon and that his system is dead wrong. You are not necessarily menacing him by stirring up this cauldron of discontent and warming envy into strife, but you are doing this: you are getting yourself on a well-greased chute that will give you a quick ride down and out. When you say to other employees that the Old Man is a curmudgeon, you reveal the fact that you are one; and when you tell them that the policy of the institution is "rotten," you certainly show that yours is.

This bad habit of fault-finding, criticising and complaining is a tool that grows keener by constant use, and there is grave danger that he who at first is only a moderate kicker may develop into a chronic knocker, and the knife he has sharpened will sever his head.

Hooker got his promotion even in spite of his many failings; but the chances are that your employer does not have the love that Lincoln had—the love that suffereth long and is kind. But even Lincoln could not protect Hooker forever. Hooker failed to do the work, and Lincoln had to try some one else. So there came a time when Hooker was superseded by a Silent Man, who criticised no one, railed at nobody –not even the enemy.

And this Silent Man, who could rule his own spirit, took the cities. He minded his own business, and did the work that no man can ever do unless he constantly gives absolute loyalty, perfect confidence, unswerving fidelity and untiring devotion. Let us mind our own business, and allow others to mind theirs, thus working for self by working for the good of all.

THE WEEK-DAY, KEEP IT HOLY

DID it ever strike you that it is a most absurd and semi-barbaric thing to set one day apart as "holy?"

If you are a writer and a beautiful thought comes to you, you never hesitate because it is Sunday, but you write it down.

If you are a painter, and the picture appears before you, vivid and clear, you make haste to materialize it ere the vision fades.

If you are a musician, you sing a song, or play it on the piano, that it may be etched upon your memory—and for the joy of it.

But if you are a cabinet-maker, you may make a design, but you will have to halt before you make the table, if the day happens to be the "Lord's Day"; and if you are a blacksmith, you will not dare to lift a hammer, for fear of conscience or the police. All of which is an admission that we regard manual labor as a sort of necessary evil, and must be done only at certain times and places.

The orthodox reason for abstinence from all manual labor on Sunday is that "God made the heavens and the earth in six days and on the seventh He rested," therefore, man, created in the image of his Maker, should hold this day sacred. How it can be possible for a supreme, omnipotent and all-powerful being without "body, parts or passions" to become wearied thru physical exertion is a question that is as yet unanswered.

The idea of serving God on Sunday and then forgetting Him all the week is a fallacy that is fostered by the Reverend Doctor Sayles and his coadjutor, Deacon Buffum, who passes the Panama for the benefit of those who would buy absolution. Or, if you prefer, salvation being free, what we place in the Panama is an honorarium for Deity or his agent, just as our noted authors never speak at banquets for pay, but accept the honorarium that in some occult and mysterious manner is left on the mantel. Sunday, with its immunity from work, was devised for slaves who got out of all the work they could during the week.

Then, to tickle the approbativeness of the slave, it was declared a virtue not to work on Sunday, a most pleasing bit of Tom Sawyer diplomacy. By following his inclinations and doing nothing, a mysterious, skyey benefit accrues, which the lazy man hopes to have and to hold for eternity.

Then the slaves who do no work on Sunday, point out those who do as beneath them in virtue, and deserving of contempt. Upon this theory all laws which punish the person who works or plays on Sunday have been passed. Does God cease work one day in seven, or is the work that He does on Sunday especially different from that which He performs on Tuesday? The Saturday half-holiday is not "sacred"—the Sunday holiday is, and we have laws to punish those who "violate" it. No man can violate the Sabbath; he can, however, violate his own nature, and this he is more apt to do through enforced idleness than either work or play. Only running water is pure, and stagnant nature of any sort is dangerous—a breeding-place for disease.

Change of occupation is necessary to mental and physical health. As it is, most people get too much of one kind of work. All the week they are chained to a task, a repugnant task because the dose is too big. They have to do this particular job or starve. This is slavery, quite as much as when man was bought and sold as a chattel.

Will there not come a time when all men and women will work because it is a blessed gift—a privilege? Then, if all worked, wasteful consuming as a business would cease. As it is, there are many people who do not work at all, and these pride themselves upon it and uphold the Sunday laws. If the idlers would work, nobody would be overworked. If this time ever comes shall we not cease to regard it as "wicked" to work at certain times, just as much as we would count it absurd to pass a law making it illegal for us to be happy on Wednesday? Isn't good work an effort to produce a useful, necessary or beautiful thing? If so, good work is a prayer, prompted by a loving heart—a prayer to benefit and bless. If prayer is not a desire, backed up by a right human effort to bring about its efficacy, then what is it?

Work is a service performed for ourselves and others. If I love you I will surely work for you—in this way I reveal my love. And to manifest my love in this manner is a joy and gratification to me. Thus work is for the worker alone and labor is its own reward. These things being true, if it is wrong to work on Sunday, it is wrong to love on Sunday; every smile is a sin, every caress a curse, and all tenderness a crime.

Must there not come a time, if we grow in mentality and spirit, when we shall cease to differentiate and quit calling some work secular and some sacred? Isn't it as necessary for me to hoe corn and feed my loved ones (and also the priest) as for the priest to preach and pray? Would any priest ever preach and pray if somebody didn't hoe? If life is from God, then all useful effort is divine; and to work is the highest form of religion. If God made us, surely He is pleased to see that His work is a success. If we are miserable, willing to liberate life with a bare bodkin, we certainly do not compliment our Maker in thus proclaiming His work a failure. But if our lives are full of gladness and we are grateful for the feeling that we are one with Deity—helping God to do His work, then, and only then do we truly serve Him.

Isn't it strange that men should have made laws declaring that it is wicked for us to work?

Exclusive Friendships

An excellent and gentle man of my acquaintance has said, "When fifty-one per cent of the voters believe in cooeperation as opposed to competition, the Ideal Commonwealth will cease to be a theory and become a fact."

That men should work together for the good of all is very beautiful, and I believe the day will come when these things will be, but the simple process of fifty-one per cent of the voters casting ballots for socialism will not bring it about.

The matter of voting is simply the expression of a sentiment, and after the ballots have been counted there still remains the work to be done. A man might vote right and act like a fool the rest of the year.

The socialist who is full of bitterness, fight, faction and jealousy is creating an opposition that will hold him and all others like him in check. And this opposition is well, for even a very imperfect society is forced to protect itself against dissolution and a condition which is worse. To take over the monopolies and operate them for the good of society is not enough, and not desirable either, so long as the idea of rivalry is rife.

As long as self is uppermost in the minds of men, they will fear and hate other men, and under socialism there would be precisely the same scramble for place and power that we see in politics now.

Society can never be reconstructed until its individual members are reconstructed. Man must be born again. When fifty-one per cent of the voters rule their own spirit and have put fifty-one per cent of their present envy, jealousy, bitterness, hate, fear and foolish pride out of their hearts, then Christian socialism will be at hand, and not until then.

The subject is entirely too big to dispose of in a paragraph, so I am just going to content myself here with the mention of one thing, that so far as I know has never been mentioned in print—the danger to society of exclusive friendships between man and man, and woman and woman. No two persons of the same sex can complement each other, neither can they long uplift or benefit each other. Usually they deform the mental and spiritual estate. We should have many acquaintances or none. When two men begin to "tell each other everything," they are hiking for senility. There must be a bit of well-defined reserve. We are told that in matter—solid steel for instance—the molecules never touch. They never surrender their individuality. We are all molecules of Divinity, and our personality should not be abandoned. Be yourself, let no man be necessary to you—your friend will think more of you if you keep him at a little distance. Friendship, like credit, is highest where it is not used.

I can understand how a strong man can have a great and abiding affection for a thousand other men, and call them all by name, but how he can regard any one of these men much higher than another and preserve his mental balance, I do not know.

Let a man come close enough and he'll clutch you like a drowning person, and down you both go. In a close and exclusive friendship men partake of others' weaknesses.

In shops and factories it happens constantly that men will have their chums. These men relate to each other their troubles—they keep nothing back—they sympathize with each other, they mutually condole.

They combine and stand by each other. Their friendship is exclusive and others see that it is. Jealousy creeps in, suspicion awakens, hate crouches around the corner, and these men combine in mutual dislike for certain things and persons. They foment each other, and their sympathy dilutes sanity—by recognizing their troubles men make them real. Things get out of focus, and the sense of values is lost. By thinking some one is an enemy you evolve him into one.

Soon others are involved and we have a clique. A clique is a friendship gone to seed.

A clique develops into a faction, and a faction into a feud, and soon we have a mob, which is a blind, stupid, insane, crazy, ramping and roaring mass that has lost the rudder. In a mob there are no individuals—all are of one mind, and independent thought is gone.

A feud is founded on nothing—it is a mistake—a fool idea fanned into flame by a fool friend! And it may become a mob.

Every man who has had anything to do with communal life has noticed that the clique is the disintegrating bacillus—and the clique has its rise always in the exclusive friendship of two persons of the same sex, who tell each other all unkind things that are said of each other—"so be on your guard." Beware of the exclusive friendship! Respect all men and try to find the good in all. To associate only with the sociable, the witty, the wise, the brilliant, is a blunder—go among the plain, the stupid, the uneducated, and exercise your own wit and wisdom. You grow by giving—have no favorites—you hold your friend as much by keeping away from him as you do by following after him.

Revere him—yes, but be natural and let space intervene. Be a Divine molecule.

Be yourself and give your friend a chance to be himself. Thus do you benefit him, and in benefiting him you benefit yourself.

The finest friendships are between those who can do without each other.

Of course there have been cases of exclusive friendship that are pointed out to us as grand examples of affection, but they are so rare and exceptional that they serve to emphasize the fact that it is exceedingly unwise for men of ordinary power and intellect to exclude their fellow men. A few men, perhaps, who are big enough to have a place in history, could play the part of David to another's Jonathan and yet retain the good will of all, but the most of us would engender bitterness and strife.

And this beautiful dream of socialism, where each shall work for the good of all, will never come about until fifty-one per cent of the adults shall abandon all exclusive friendships. Until that day arrives you will have cliques, denominations—which are cliques grown big—factions, feuds and occasional mobs.

Do not lean on any one, and let no one lean on you. The ideal society will be made up of ideal individuals. Be a man and be a friend to everybody.

When the Master admonished his disciples to love their enemies, he had in mind the truth that an exclusive love is a mistake—love dies when it is monopolized—it grows by giving. Love, lim., is an error. Your enemy is one who misunderstands you—why should you not rise above the fog and see his error and respect him for the good qualities you find in him?

The Folly of Living in the Future

The question is often asked, "What becomes of all the Valedictorians and all the Class-Day Poets?"

I can give information as to two parties for whom this inquiry is made—the Valedictorian of my class is now a most industrious and worthy floor-walker in Siegel, Cooper & Company's store, and I was the Class-Day Poet. Both of us had our eyes fixed on the Goal. We stood on the Threshold and looked out upon the World preparatory to going forth, seizing it by the tail and snapping its head off for our own delectation.

We had our eyes fixed on the Goal—it might better have been the gaol.

It was a very absurd thing for us to fix our eyes on the Goal. It strained our vision and took our attention from our work. We lost our grip on the present.

To think of the Goal is to travel the distance over and over in your mind and dwell on how awfully far off it is. We have so little mind—doing business on such a limited capital of intellect—that to wear it threadbare looking for a far-off thing is to get hopelessly stranded in Siegel, Cooper & Company.

Of course, Siegel, Cooper & Company is all right, too, but the point is this—it wasn't the Goal!

A goodly dash of indifference is a requisite in the formula for doing a great work.

No one knows what the Goal is—we are all sailing under sealed orders.

Do your work to-day, doing it the best you can, and live one day at a time. The man that does this is conserving his God-given energy, and not spinning it out into tenuous spider threads so fragile and filmy that unkind Fate will probably brush it away.

To do your work well to-day, is the certain preparation for something better to-morrow. The past has gone from us forever; the future we cannot reach; the present alone is ours. Each day's work is a preparation for the next day's duties.

Live in the present—the Day is here, the time is Now.

There is only one thing that is worth praying for—that we may be in the line of Evolution.

THE SPIRIT OF MAN

Maybe I am all wrong about it, yet I cannot help believing that the spirit of man will live again in a better world than ours. Fenelon says: "Justice demands another life to make good the inequalities of this." Astronomers prophesy the existence of stars long before they can see them. They know where they ought to be, and training their telescopes in that direction they wait, knowing they shall find them.

Materially, no one can imagine anything more beautiful than this earth, for the simple reason that we cannot imagine anything we have not seen; we may make new combinations, but the whole is made up of parts of things with which we are familiar. This great green earth out of which we have sprung, of which we are a part, that supports our bodies which must return to it to repay the loan, is very, very beautiful.

But the spirit of man is not fully at home here; as we grow in soul and intellect, we hear, and hear again, a voice which says: "Arise and get thee hence, for this is not thy rest." And the greater and nobler and more sublime the spirit, the more constant is the discontent. Discontent may come from various causes, so it will not do to assume that the discontented ones are always the pure in heart, but it is a fact that the wise and excellent have all known the meaning of world-weariness. The more you study and appreciate this life, the more sure you are that this is not all. You pillow your head upon Mother Earth, listen to her heart-throb, and even as your spirit is filled with the love of her, your gladness is half pain and there comes to you a joy that hurts. To look upon the most exalted forms of beauty, such as sunset at sea, the coming of a storm on the prairie, or the sublime majesty of the mountains, begets a sense of sadness, an increasing loneliness. It is not enough to say that man encroaches on man so that we are really deprived of our freedom, that civilization is caused by a bacillus, and that from a natural condition we have gotten into a hurly-burly where rivalry is rife—all this may be true, but beyond and outside of all this there is no physical environment in way of plenty which earth can supply, that will give the tired soul peace. They are the happiest who have the least; and the fable of the stricken king and the shirtless beggar contains the germ of truth. The wise hold all earthly ties very lightly—they are stripping for eternity.

World-weariness is only a desire for a better spiritual condition. There is more to be written on this subject of world-pain—to exhaust the theme would require a book. And certain it is that I have no wish to say the final word on any topic. The gentle reader has certain rights, and among these is the privilege of summing up the case.

But the fact holds that world-pain is a form of desire. All desires are just, proper and right; and their gratification is the means by which nature supplies us that which we need.

Desire not only causes us to seek that which we need, but is a form of attraction by which the good is brought to us, just as the amoebae create a swirl in the waters that brings their food within reach.

Every desire in nature has a fixed and definite purpose in the Divine Economy, and every desire has its proper gratification. If we desire the close friendship of a certain person, it is because that person has certain soul-qualities that we do not possess, and which complement our own.

Through desire do we come into possession of our own; by submitting to its beckonings we add cubits to our stature; and we also give out to others our own attributes, without becoming poorer, for soul is not limited. All nature is a symbol of spirit, and so I am forced to believe that somewhere there must be a proper gratification for this mysterious nostalgia of thc soul.

The Valhalla of the Norseman, the Nirvana of the Hindu, the Heaven of the Christian are natural hopes of beings whose cares and disappointments here are softened by belief that somewhere, Thor, Brahma or God gives compensation.

The Eternal Unities require a condition where men and women shall be permitted to love and not to sorrow; where the tyranny of things hated shall not prevail, nor that for which the heart yearns turn to ashes at our touch.

ART AND RELIGION

WHILE this seems true in the main, I am not sure it will hold in every case. Please think it out for yourself, and if I happen to be wrong, why, put me straight.

The proposition is this: the artist needs no religion beyond his work. That is to say, art is religion to the man who thinks beautiful thoughts and expresses them for others the best he can. Religion is an emotional excitement whereby the devotee rises into a state of spiritual sublimity, and for the moment is bathed in an atmosphere of rest, and peace, and love. All normal men and women crave such periods; and Bernard Shaw says that we reach them through strong tea, tobacco, whiskey, opium, love, art or religion.

I think Bernard Shaw a cynic, but there is a glimmer of truth in his idea that makes it worth repeating. But beyond the natural religion, which is a passion for oneness with the Whole, all formalized religions engraft the element of fear, and teach the necessity of placating a Supreme Being. Our idea of a Supreme Being is suggested to us by the political government under which we live. The situation was summed up by Carlyle, when he said that Deity to the average British mind was simply an infinite George IV. The thought of God as a terrible Supreme Tyrant first found form in an unlimited monarchy; but as governments have become more lenient so have the gods, until you get them down (or up) to a republic, where God is only a president, and we all approach Him in familiar prayer, on an absolute equality.

Then soon, for the first time, we find man saying, "I am God, and you are God, and we are all simply particles of Him," and this is where the president is done away with, and the referendum comes in. But the absence of a supreme governing head implies simplicity, honesty, justice, and sincerity. Wherever plottings, schemings and doubtful methods of life are employed, a ruler is necessary; and there, too, religion, with its idea of placating God has a firm hold. Men whose lives are doubtful feel the need of a strong government and a hot religion. Formal religion and sin go hand in hand. Formal religion and slavery go hand in hand. Formal religion and tyranny go hand in hand. Formal religion and ignorance go hand in hand.

And sin, slavery, tyranny and ignorance are one—they are never separated.

Formal religion is a scheme whereby man hopes to make peace with his Maker; and a formal religion also tends to satisfy the sense of sublimity where the man has failed to find satisfaction in his work. Voltaire says, "When woman no longer finds herself acceptable to man, she turns to God," When man is no longer acceptable to himself he goes to church. In order to keep this article from extending itself into a tome, I purposely omitted saying a single thing about the Protestant Church as a useful Social Club and have just assumed for argument's sake that the church is really a religious institution.

A formal religion is only a cut 'cross lots—an attempt to bring about the emotions and the sensations that come to a man by the practice of love, virtue, excellence and truth. When you do a splendid piece of work and express your best, there comes to you, as reward, an exaltation of soul, a sublimity of feeling that puts you for the time being in touch with the Infinite. A formal religion brings this feeling without your doing anything useful, therefore it is unnatural.

Formalized religion is the strongest where sin, slavery, tyranny and ignorance abound. Where men are free, enlightened and at work, they find all the gratification in their work that their souls demand—they cease to hunt outside themselves for something to give them rest. They are at peace with themselves, at peace with man and with God.

But any man chained to a hopeless task, whose daily work does not express himself, who is dogged by a boss, whenever he gets a moment of respite turns to drink or religion.

Men with an eye on Saturday night, who plot to supplant some one else, who can locate an employer any hour of the day, who use their wit to evade labor, who think only of their summer vacation when they will no longer be compelled to work, are apt to be sticklers for Sabbath-keeping and church-going.

Gentlemen in business who give eleven for a dozen, and count thirty-four inches a yard, who are quick to foreclose a mortgage, and who say "business is business," generally are vestrymen, deacons and church trustees. Look about you! Predaceous real estate dealers who set nets for all the unwary, lawyers who lie in wait for their prey, merchant princes who grind their clerks under the wheel, and oil magnates whose history was never written, nor could be written, often make peace with God, and find a gratification for their sense of sublimity by building churches, founding colleges, giving libraries, and holding firmly to a formalized religion. Look about you!

To recapitulate: if your life-work is doubtful, questionable or distasteful, you will hold the balance true by going outside your vocation for the gratification that is your due, but which your daily work denies, and you find it in religion, I do not say this is always so, but it is very often. Great sinners are apt to be very religious; and conversely, the best men who have ever lived have been at war with established religions. And further, the best men are never found in churches.

Men deeply immersed in their work, whose lives are consecrated to doing things, who are simple, honest and sincere, desire no formal religion, need no priest nor pastor, and seek no gratification outside their daily lives. All they ask is to be let alone—they wish only the privilege to work.

When Samuel Johnson, on his death bed, made Joshua Reynolds promise he would do no more work on Sunday, he of course had no conception of the truth that Reynolds reached through work the same condition of mind that he, Johnson, had reached by going to church. Johnson despised work and Reynolds loved it; Johnson considered one day in the week holy; to Reynolds all days were sacred—sacred to work; that is, to the expression of his best. Why should you cease to express your holiest and highest on Sunday? Ah, I know why you don't work on Sunday! It is because you think that work is degrading, and because your sale and barter is founded on fraud, and your goods are shoddy. Your week-day dealings lie like a pall upon your conscience, and you need a day in which to throw off the weariness of that slavery under which you live. You are not free yourself, and you insist that others shall not be free.

You have ceased to make work gladsome, and you toil and make others toil with you, and you all well nigh faint from weariness and disgust. You are slave and slave-owner, for to own slaves is to be one.

But the artist is free and he works in joy, and to him all things are good and all days are holy. The great inventors, thinkers, poets, musicians and artists have all been men of deep religious natures; but their religion has never been a formalized, restricted, ossified religion. They did not worship at set times and places. Their religion has been a natural and spontaneous blossoming of the intellect and emotions—they have worked in love, not only one day in the week, but all days, and to them the groves have always and ever been God's first temples.

Let us work to make men free! Am I bad because I want to give you freedom, and have you work in gladness instead of fear?

Do not hesitate to work on Sunday, just as you would think good thoughts if the spirit prompts you. For work is, at the last, only the expression of your thought, and there can be no better religion than good work.

Initiative

The world bestows its big prizes, both in money and honors, for but one thing. And that is Initiative. What is Initiative? I'll tell you: It is doing the right thing without being told. But next to doing the right thing without being told is to do it when you are told once. That is to say, carry the Message to Garcia! There are those who never do a thing until they are told twice: such get no honors and small pay. Next, there are those who do the right thing only when necessity kicks them from behind, and these get indifference instead of honors, and a pittance for pay. This kind spends most of its time polishing a bench with a hard-luck story. Then, still lower down in the scale than this, we find the fellow who will not do the right thing even when some one goes along to show him how, and stays to see that he does it; he is always out of a job, and receives the contempt he deserves, unless he has a rich Pa, in which case Destiny awaits near by with a stuffed club. To which class do you belong?

THE DISAGREEABLE GIRL

England's most famous dramatist, George Bernard Shaw, has placed in the pillory of letters what he is pleased to call "The Disagreeable Girl."

And he has done it by a dry-plate, quick-shutter process in a manner that surely lays him liable for criminal libel in the assize of high society.

I say society's assize advisedly, because it is only in society that the Disagreeable Girl can play a prominent part, assuming the center of the stage. Society, in the society sense, is built upon vacuity; its favors being for those who reveal a fine capacity to waste and consume. Those who would write their names high on society's honor roll, need not be either useful or intelligent—they need only seem.

And this gives to the Disagreeable Girl her opportunity. In the paper box factory she would have to make good; Cluett, Coon & Co. ask for results; the stage demands at least a modicum of intellect, in addition to shape, but society asks for nothing but pretense, and the palm is awarded to palaver. But do not, if you please, imagine that the Disagreeable Girl does not wield an influence. That is the very point—her influence is so far-reaching in its effect that George Bernard Shaw, giving cross-sections of life in the form of dramas, cannot write a play and leave her out.

She is always with us, ubiquitous, omniscient and omnipresent—is the Disagreeable Girl. She is a disappointment to her father, a source of humiliation to her mother, a pest to her brothers and sisters, and when she finally marries, she slowly saps the inspiration of her husband and very often converts a proud and ambitious man into a weak and cowardly cur.

Only in society does the Disagreeable Girl shine—everywhere else she is an abject failure. The much-vaunted Gibson Girl is a kind of de luxe edition of Shaw's Disagreeable Girl. The Gibson Girl lolls, loafs, pouts, weeps, talks back, lies in wait, dreams, eats, drinks, sleeps and yawns. She rides in a coach in a red jacket, plays golf in a secondary sexual sweater, dawdles on a hotel veranda, and can tum-tum on a piano, but you never hear of her doing a useful thing or saying a wise one. She plays bridge whist, for "keeps" when she wins, and "owes" when she loses, and her picture in flattering half-tone often adorns a page of the Sunday Yellow.

She reveals a beautiful capacity for avoiding all useful effort.

Gibson gilds the Disagreeable Girl.

Shaw paints her as she is.

In the *Doll's House* Henrik Ibsen has given us *Nora Hebler,* a Disagreeable Girl of mature age, who, beyond a doubt, first set George Bernard Shaw a-thinking.

Then looking about, Shaw saw her at every turn in every stage of her moth-and-butterfly existence.

And the Disagreeable Girl being everywhere, Shaw, dealer in human character, cannot write a play and leave her out, any more than the artist Turner could paint a picture and leave man out, or Paul Veronese produce a canvas and omit the dog.

The Disagreeable Girl is a female of the genus homo persuasion, built around a digestive apparatus that possesses marked marshmallow proclivities. She is pretty, pug-nosed, pink, pert and poetical; and at first glance, to the unwary, she shows signs of gentleness and intelligence. Her age is anywhere from eighteen to twenty-eight. At twenty-eight she begins to evolve into something else, and her capacity for harm is largely curtailed, because by this time spirit has written itself in her form and features, and the grossness and animality which before were veiled are becoming apparent.

Habit writes itself on the face, and body is an automatic recording machine.

To have a beautiful old age, you must live a beautiful youth, for we ourselves are posterity, and every man is his own ancestor. I am to-day what I am because I was yesterday what I was. The Disagreeable Girl is always pretty, at least we have been told she is pretty, and she fully accepts the dictum.

She has also been told she is clever, and she thinks she is.

The actual fact is she is only "sassy."

The fine flaring up of youth has tended to set sex rampant, but she is not "immoral" save in her mind.

She has caution to the verge of cowardice, and so she is sans reproche. In public she pretends to be dainty; but alone, or with those for whose good opinion she does not care, she is gross, coarse and sensual in every feature of her life. She eats too much, does not exercise enough and considers it amusing to let other people wait on her and do for her the things she should do for herself. Her room is a jumble of disorder. The one gleam of hope for her lies in the fact that out of shame, she allows no visitor to enter her apartments if she can help it. Concrete selfishness is her chief mark. She will avoid responsibility, side-step every duty that calls for honest effort; is untruthful, secretive, indolent and dishonest.

"What are you eating?" asks Nora Hebler's husband as she enters the room, not expecting to see him.

"Nothing," is the answer, and she hides the box of bonbons behind her, and soon backs out of the room.

I think Mr. Hebler had no business to ask her what she was eating—no man should ask any woman such a question, and really it was no difference anyway. But Nora is always on the defensive and fabricates when it is necessary, and when it isn't, just through habit. She will hide a letter written by her grandmother as quickly and deftly as if it were a missive from a guilty lover. The habit of her life is one of suspicion, for being inwardly guilty herself, she suspects everybody although it is quite likely that crime with her has never broken through thought into deed. Nora will rifle her husband's pockets, read his note-book, examine his letters, and when he goes on a trip she spends the day checking up his desk, for her soul delights in duplicate keys.

At times she lets drop hints of knowledge concerning little nothings that are none of hers, just to mystify folks.

She does strange, annoying things simply to see what others will do.

In degree, Nora's husband fixed the vice of finesse in her nature, for when even a "good" woman is accused she parries by the use of trickery and wins her point by the artistry of the bagnio. Women and men are never really far apart anyway, and women are largely what men have made them.

We are all just getting rid of our shackles; listen closely, anywhere, even among honest and intellectual people, if such there be, and you can detect the rattle of chains.

The Disagreeable Girl's mind and soul have not kept pace with her body. Yesterday she was a slave, sold in a Circassian mart, and freedom to her is so new and strange that she is unfamiliar with her environment, and she does not know what to do with it.

The tragedy she works, according to George Bernard Shaw, is through the fact that very often good men, blinded by the glamour of sex, imagine they love the Disagreeable Girl, when what they love is their own ideal—an image born in their own minds.

Nature is both a trickster and a humorist, and ever sets the will of the species beyond the discernment of the individual. The picador has to blindfold his horse in order to get him into the bull-ring, and likewise, Dan Cupid does the myopic to a purpose.

For aught we know, the lovely Beatrice of Dante was only a Disagreeable Girl, clothed in a poet's fancy, and idealized by a dreamer. Fortunate was Dante that he worshipped her afar, that he never knew her well enough to be undeceived, and so walked through life in love with love, sensitive, saintly, sweetly sad and most divinely happy in his melancholy.

THE NEUTRAL

THERE is known to me a prominent business house that by the very force of its directness and worth has incurred the enmity of many rivals. In fact, there is a very general conspiracy on hand to put the institution down and out. In talking with a young man employed by this house, he yawned and said, "Oh, in this quarrel I am neutral."

"But you get your bread and butter from this firm, and in a matter where the very life of the institution is concerned, I do not see how you can be a neutral."

And he changed the subject.

I think that if I enlisted in the Japanese army I would not be a neutral.

Business is a fight—a continual struggle—just as life is. Man has reached his present degree of development through struggle. Struggle there must be and always will be. The struggle began as purely physical;

as man evolved it shifted ground to the mental, psychic, and the spiritual, with a few dashes of cave-man proclivities still left. But depend upon it, the struggle will always be—life is activity. And when it gets to be a struggle in well-doing, it will still be a struggle. When inertia gets the better of you it is time to telephone to the undertaker.

The only real neutral in this game of life is a dead one.

Eternal vigilance is not only the price of liberty, but of every other good thing.

A business that is not safeguarded on every side by active, alert, attentive, vigilant men is gone. As oxygen is the disintegrating principle of life, working night and day to dissolve, separate, pull apart and dissipate, so there is something in business that continually tends to scatter, destroy and shift possession from this man to that. A million mice nibble eternally at every business venture.

The mice are not neutrals, and if enough employes in a business house are neutrals, the whole concern will eventually come tumbling about their ears.

I like that order of Field-Marshal Oyama: "Give every honorable neutral that you find in our lines the honorable jiu-jitsu hikerino."

REFLECTIONS ON PROGRESS

Renan has said that truth is always rejected when it comes to a man for the first time, its evolution being as follows:

First, we say the thing is rank heresy, and contrary to the Bible.

Second, we say the matter really amounts to nothing, anyway.

Third, we declare that we always believed it.

Two hundred years ago partnerships in business were very rare. A man in business simply made things and sold them—and all the manufacturing was done by himself and his immediate family. Soon we find instances of brothers continuing the work the father had begun, as in the case of the Elzevirs and the Plantins, the great bookmakers of Holland. To meet this competition, four printers, in 1640, formed a partnership and pooled their efforts. A local writer by the name of

Van Krugen denounced these four men, and made savage attacks on partnerships in general as wicked and illegal, and opposed to the best interests of the people. This view seems to have been quite general, for there was a law in Amsterdam forbidding all partnerships in business that were not licensed by the state. The legislature of the State of Missouri has recently made war on the department store in the same way, using the ancient Van Krugen argument as a reason, for there is no copyright on stupidity.

In London in the seventeenth century men who were found guilty of pooling their efforts and dividing profits, were convicted by law and punished for "contumacy, contravention and connivance," and were given a taste of the stocks in the public square.

When corporations were formed for the first time, only a few years ago, there was a fine burst of disapproval. The corporation was declared a scheme of oppression, a hungry octopus, a grinder of the individual. And to prove the case various instances of hardship were cited; and no doubt there was much suffering, for many people are never able to adjust themselves to new conditions without experiencing pain and regret.

But we now believe that corporations came because they were required. Certain things the times demanded, and no one man, or two or three men could perform these tasks alone—hence the corporation. The rise of England as a manufacturing nation began with the plan of the stock company.

The aggregation known as the joint-stock company, everybody is willing now to admit, was absolutely necessary in order to secure the machinery, that is to say, the tools, the raw stock, the buildings, and to provide for the permanence of the venture.

The railroad system of America has built up this country—on this thing of joint-stock companies and transportation, our prosperity has hinged. "Commerce, consists in carrying things from where they are plentiful to where they are needed," says Emerson.

There are ten combinations of capital in this country that control over six thousand miles of railroad each. These companies have taken in a large number of small lines; and many connecting lines of tracks have been built. Competition over vast sections of country has been practically obliterated, and this has been done so quietly that few people are aware of the change. Only one general result of this consolidation of management has been felt, and that it is better service at less expense. No captain of any great industrial enterprise dares now to say, "The public be damned," even if he ever said it—which I much doubt. The pathway to success lies in serving the public, not in affronting it. In no other way is success possible, and this truth is so plain and patent that even very simple folk are able to recognize it. You can only help yourself by helping others.

Thirty years ago, when P. T. Barnum said, "The public delights in being humbugged," he knew that it was not true, for he never attempted to put the axiom in practice. He amused the public by telling it a lie, but P. T. Barnum never tried anything so risky as deception. Even when he lied we were not deceived; truth can be stated by indirection. "When my love tells me she is made of truth, I do believe her, though I know she lies." Barnum always gave more than he advertised; and going over and over the same territory he continued to amuse and instruct the public for nearly forty years.

This tendency to cooeperate is seen in such splendid features as the Saint Louis Union Station, for instance, where just twenty great railroad companies lay aside envy, prejudice, rivalry and whim, and use one terminal. If competition were really the life of trade, each railroad that enters Saint Louis would have a station of its own, and the public would be put to the worry, trouble, expense and endless delay of finding where it wanted to go and how to get there. As it is now, the entire aim and end of the scheme is to reduce friction, worry and expense, and give the public the greatest accommodation—the best possible service—to make travel easy and life secure. Servants in uniform meet you as you alight, and answer your every question—speeding you courteously and kindly on your way. There are women to take care of women, and nurses to take care of children, and wheel chairs for such as may be infirm or lame. The intent is to serve—not to pull you this way and that, and sell you a ticket over a certain road. You are free to choose your route and you are free to utilize as your own this great institution that cost a million dollars, and that requires the presence of two hundred people to maintain. All is for you. It is for the public and was only made possible by a oneness of aim and desire—that is to say cooeperation. Before cooeperation comes in any line, there is always competition pushed to a point that threatens destruction and promises chaos; then to divert ruin, men devise a better way, a plan that conserves and economizes, and behold, it is found in cooeperation.

Civilization is an evolution.

Civilization is not a thing separate and apart, any more than art is.

Art is the beautiful way of doing things. Civilization is the expeditious way of doing things. And as haste is often waste—the more hurry the less speed—civilization is the best way of doing things.

As mankind multiplies in number, the problem of supplying people what they need is the important question of Earth. And mankind has ever held out offers of reward in fame and money—both being forms of power—to those who would supply it better things.

Teachers are those who educate the people to appreciate the things they need.

The man who studies mankind, and finds out what men really want, and then supplies them this, whether it be an Idea or a Thing, is the man who is crowned with the laurel wreath of honor and clothed with riches.

What people need and what they want may be very different.

To undertake to supply people a thing you think they need but which they do not want, is to have your head elevated on a pike, and your bones buried in Potter's Field.

But wait, and the world will yet want the thing that it needs, and your bones will then become sacred relics.

This change in desire on the part of mankind is the result of the growth of intellect.

It is Progress, and Progress is Evolution, and Evolution is Progress.

There are men who are continually trying to push Progress along: we call these individuals "Reformers."

Then there are others who always oppose the Reformer—the mildest name we have for them is "Conservative."

The Reformer is either a Savior or a Rebel, all depending on whether he succeeds or fails, and your point of view. He is what he is, regardless of what other men think of him. The man who is indicted and executed as a rebel, often afterward has the word "Savior" carved on his tomb; and sometimes men who are hailed as saviors in their day are afterward found to be sham saviors—to wit, charlatans. Conservation is a plan of Nature. To keep the good is to conserve. A Conservative is a man who puts on the brakes when he thinks Progress is going to land Civilization in the ditch and wreck the whole concern.

Brakemen are necessary, but in the language of Koheleth, there is a time to apply the brake and there is a time to abstain from applying the brake. To clog the wheels continually is to stand still, and to stand still is to retreat. Progress has need of the brakeman, but the brakeman should not occupy all of his time putting on the brakes.

The Conservative is just as necessary as the Radical. The Conservative keeps the Reformer from going too fast, and plucking the fruit before it is ripe. Governments are only good where there is strong Opposition, just as the planets are held in place by the opposition of forces. And so civilization goes forward by stops and starts—pushed by the Reformers and held back by the Conservatives. One is necessary to the other, and they often shift places. But forward and forward Civilization forever goes—ascertaining the best way of doing things.

In commerce we have had the Individual Worker, the Partnership, the Corporation, and now we have the Trust.

The Trust is simply Corporations forming a partnership. The thing is all an Evolution—a moving forward. It is all for man and it is all done by man. It is all done with the consent, aye, and approval of man.

The Trusts were made by the People, and the People can and will unmake them, should they ever prove an engine of oppression. They exist only during good behavior, and like men, they are living under a sentence of death, with an indefinite reprieve.

The Trusts are good things because they are economizers of energy. They cut off waste, increase the production, and make a panic practically impossible.

The Trusts are here in spite of the men who think they originated them, and in spite of the Reformers who turned Conservatives and opposed them.

The next move of Evolution will be the age of Socialism. Socialism means the operation of all industries by the people, and for the people. Socialism is cooeperation instead of competition. Competition has been so general that economists mistook it for a law of nature, when it was only an incident.

Competition is no more a law of nature than is hate. Hate was once so thoroughly believed in that we gave it personality and called it the Devil.

We have banished the Devil by educating people to know that he who works has no time to hate and no need to fear, and by this same means, education, will the people be prepared for the age of Socialism.

The Trusts are now getting things ready for Socialism.

Socialism is a Trust of Trusts.

Humanity is growing in intellect, in patience, in kindness—in love. And when the time is ripe, the people will step in and take peaceful possession of their own, and the Cooeperative Commonwealth will give to each one his due.

SYMPATHY, KNOWLEDGE AND POISE

SYMPATHY, Knowledge and Poise seem to be the three ingredients that are most needed in forming the Gentle Man. I place these elements according to their value. No man is great who does not have Sympathy plus, and the greatness of men can be safely gauged by their sympathies. Sympathy and imagination are twin sisters. Your heart must go out to all men, the high, the low, the rich, the poor, the learned, the unlearned, the good, the bad, the wise and the foolish—it is necessary to be one with them all, else you can never comprehend them. Sympathy!—it is the touchstone to every secret, the key to all knowledge, the open sesame of all hearts. Put yourself in the other man's place and then you will know why he thinks certain things and does certain deeds. Put yourself in his place and your blame will dissolve itself into pity, and your tears will wipe out the record of his misdeeds. The saviors of the world have simply been men with wondrous sympathy.

But Knowledge must go with Sympathy, else the emotions will become maudlin and pity may be wasted on a poodle instead of a child; on a field-mouse instead of a human soul. Knowledge in use is wisdom, and wisdom implies a sense of values—you know a big thing from a little one, a valuable fact from a trivial one. Tragedy and comedy are simply questions of value: a little misfit in life makes us laugh, a great one is tragedy and cause for expression of grief.

Poise is the strength of body and strength of mind to control your Sympathy and your Knowledge. Unless you control your emotions they run over and you stand in the mire. Sympathy must not run riot, or it is valueless and tokens weakness instead of strength. In every hospital for nervous disorders are to be found many instances of this loss of control. The individual has Sympathy but not Poise, and therefore his life is worthless to himself and to the world.

He symbols inefficiency and not helpfulness. Poise reveals itself more in voice than it does in words; more in thought than in action; more in atmosphere than in conscious life. It is a spiritual quality, and is felt more than it is seen. It is not a matter of bodily size, nor of bodily attitude, nor attire, nor of personal comeliness: it is a state of inward being, and of knowing your cause is just. And so you see it is a great and profound subject after all, great in its ramifications, limitless in extent, implying the entire science of right living. I once met a man who was deformed in body and little more than a dwarf, but who had such Spiritual Gravity—such Poise—that to enter a room where he was, was to feel his presence and acknowledge his superiority. To allow Sympathy to waste itself on unworthy objects is to deplete one's life forces. To conserve is the part of wisdom, and reserve is a necessary element in all good literature, as well as in everything else.

Poise being the control of our Sympathy and Knowledge, it implies a possession of these attributes, for without having Sympathy and Knowledge you have nothing to control but your physical body. To practise Poise as a mere gymnastic exercise, or study in etiquette, is to be self-conscious, stiff, preposterous and ridiculous. Those who cut such fantastic tricks before high heaven as make angels weep, are men void of Sympathy and Knowledge trying to cultivate Poise. Their science is a mere matter of what to do with arms and legs. Poise is a question of spirit controlling flesh, heart controlling attitude.

Get Knowledge by coming close to Nature. That man is the greatest who best serves his kind. Sympathy and Knowledge are for use—you acquire that you may give out; you accumulate that you may bestow. And as God has given unto you the sublime blessings of Sympathy and Knowledge, there will come to you the wish to reveal your gratitude by giving them out again; for the wise man is aware that we retain spiritual qualities only as we give them away. Let your light shine. To him that hath shall be given. The exercise of wisdom brings wisdom; and at the last the infinitesimal quantity of man's knowledge, compared with the Infinite, and the smallness of man's Sympathy when compared with the source from which ours is absorbed, will evolve an abnegation and a humility that will lend a perfect Poise. The Gentleman is a man with perfect Sympathy, Knowledge, and Poise.

LOVE AND FAITH

No woman is worthy to be a wife who on the day of her marriage is not lost absolutely and entirely in an atmosphere of love and perfect trust; the supreme sacredness of the relation is the only thing which, at the time, should possess her soul. Is she a bawd that she should bargain?

Women should not "obey" men anymore than men should obey women. There are six requisites in every happy marriage; the first is Faith, and the remaining five are Confidence. Nothing so compliments a man as for a woman to believe in him—nothing so pleases a woman as for a man to place confidence in her.

Obey? God help me! Yes, if I loved a woman, my whole heart's desire would be to obey her slightest wish. And how could I love her unless I had perfect confidence that she would only aspire to what was beautiful, true and right? And to enable her to realize this ideal, her wish would be to me a sacred command; and her attitude of mind toward me I know would be the same. And the only rivalry between us would be as to who could love the most; and the desire to obey would be the one controlling impulse of our lives.

We gain freedom by giving it, and he who bestows faith gets it back with interest. To bargain and stipulate in love is to lose.

The woman who stops the marriage ceremony and requests the minister to omit the word "obey," is sowing the first seed of doubt and distrust that later may come to fruition in the divorce court.

The haggling and bickerings of settlements and dowries that usually precede the marriage of "blood" and "dollars" are the unheeded warnings that misery, heartache, suffering, and disgrace await the principals.

Perfect faith implies perfect love; and perfect love casteth out fear. It is always the fear of imposition, and a lurking intent to rule, that causes the woman to haggle over a word—it is absence of love, a limitation, an incapacity. The price of a perfect love is an absolute and complete surrender.

Keep back part of the price and yours will be the fate of Ananias and Sapphira. Your doom is swift and sure. To win all we must give all.

Giving Something for Nothing

To give a man something for nothing tends to make the individual dissatisfied with himself.

Your enemies are the ones you have helped.

And when an individual is dissatisfied with himself he is dissatisfied with the whole world—and with you.

A man's quarrel with the world is only a quarrel with himself. But so strong is this inclination to lay blame elsewhere and take credit to ourselves, that when we are unhappy we say it is the fault of this woman or that man. Especially do women attribute their misery to That Man.

And often the trouble is he has given her too much for nothing.

This truth is a reversible, back-action one, well lubricated by use, working both ways—as the case may be.

Nobody but a beggar has really definite ideas concerning his rights. People who give much—who love much—do not haggle.

That form of affection which drives sharp bargains and makes demands, gets a check on the bank in which there is no balance.

There is nothing so costly as something you get for nothing.

My friend Tom Lowry, Magnate in Ordinary, of Minneapolis and the east side of Wall Street, has recently had a little experience that proves my point.

A sturdy beggar-man, a specimen of decayed gentility, once called on Tammas with a hard-luck story and a Family Bible, and asked for a small loan on the Good Book.

To be compelled to soak the Family Bible would surely melt the heart of gneiss!

Tom was melted.

Tom made the loan but refused the collateral, stating he had no use for it.

Which was God's truth for once.

In a few weeks the man came back, and tried to tell Tom his hard-luck story concerning the Cold Ingratitude of a Cruel World.

Tom said, "Spare me the slow music and the recital—I have troubles of my own. I need mirth and good cheer—take this dollar, and peace be with you."

"Peace be multiplied unto thee," said the beggar, and departed. The next month the man returned, and began to tell Tom a tale of Cruelty, Injustice and Ingratitude.

Tom was riled—he had his magnate business to attend to, and he made a remark in italics. The beggar said, "Mr. Lowry, if you had your business a little better systematized, I would not have to trouble you personally—why don't you just speak to your cashier?" And the great man, who once took a party of friends out for a tally-ho ride, and through mental habit collected five cents from each guest, was so pleased at the thought of relief that he pressed the buzzer. The cashier came, and Tom said, "Put this man Grabheimer on your payroll, give him two dollars now and the same the first of every month."

Then turning to the beggar-man, Tom said, "Now get out of here—hurry, vamose, hike—and be damned to you!"

"The same to you and many of them," said His Effluvia politely, and withdrew.

All this happened two years ago. The beggar got his money regularly for a year, and then in auditing accounts Tom found the name on the pay-roll, and as Tom could not remember how the name got there, he at first thought the pay-roll was being stuffed. Anyway he ordered the beggar's name stricken off the roster, and the elevator man was instructed to enforce the edict against beggars.

Not being allowed to see his man, the beggar wrote him letters—denunciatory, scandalous, abusive, threatening. Finally the beggar laid the matter before an obese limb o' the Law, Jaggers, of the firm of Jaggers & Jaggers, who took the case on a contingent fee.

The case came to trial, and Jaggers proved his case se offendendo—argal: it was shown by the defendant's books that His Bacteria had been on the pay-roll and his name had been stricken off without suggestion, request, cause, reason or fault of his own.

His Crabship proved the contract, and Tom got it in the mazzard. Judgment for plaintiff, with costs. The beggar got the money and Minneapolis Tom got the experience. Tom said the man would lose the money, but he himself has gotten the part that will be his for ninety-nine years. Surely the spirit of justice does not sleep and there is a beneficent and wise Providence that watches over magnates.

Work and Waste

These truths I hold to be self-evident: That man was made to be happy; that happiness is only attainable through useful effort; that the very best way to help ourselves is to help others, and often the best way to help others is to mind our own business; that useful effort means the proper exercise of all our faculties; that we grow only through exercise; that education should continue through life, and the joys of mental endeavor should be, especially, the solace of the old; that where men alternate work, play and study in right proportion, the organs of the mind are the last to fail, and death for such has no terrors.

That the possession of wealth can never make a man exempt from useful manual labor; that if all would work a little, no one would then be overworked; that if no one wasted, all would have enough; that if none were overfed, none would be underfed; that the rich and "educated" need education quite as much as the poor and illiterate; that the presence of a serving class is an indictment and a disgrace to our civilization; that the disadvantage of having a serving class falls most upon those who are served, and not upon those who serve—just as the real curse of slavery fell upon the slave-owners.

That people who are waited on by a serving class cannot have a right consideration for the rights of others, and they waste both time and substance, both of which are lost forever, and can only seemingly be made good by additional human effort.

That the person who lives on the labor of others, not giving himself in return to the best of his ability, is really a consumer of human life and therefore must be considered no better than a cannibal.

That each one living naturally will do the thing he can do best, but that in useful service there is no high nor low.

That to set apart one day in seven as "holy" is really absurd and serves only to loosen our grasp on the tangible present.

That all duties, offices and things which are useful and necessary to humanity are sacred, and that nothing else is or can be sacred.

THE LAW OF OBEDIENCE

THE very first item in the creed of common sense is *Obedience*.

Perform your work with a whole heart.

Revolt may be sometimes necessary, but the man who tries to mix revolt and obedience is doomed to disappoint himself and everybody with whom he has dealings. To flavor work with protest is to fail absolutely.

When you revolt, why revolt—climb, hike, get out, defy— tell everybody and everything to go to hades! That disposes of the case. You thus separate yourself entirely from those you have served—no one misunderstands you—you have declared yourself.

The man who quits in disgust when ordered to perform a task which he considers menial or unjust may be a pretty good fellow, but in the wrong environment, but the malcontent who takes your order with a smile and then secretly disobeys, is a dangerous proposition. To pretend to obey, and yet carry in your heart the spirit of revolt is to do half-hearted, slipshod work. If revolt and obedience are equal in power, your engine will then stop on the center and you benefit no one, not even yourself.

The spirit of obedience is the controlling impulse that dominates the receptive mind and the hospitable heart. There are boats that mind the helm and there are boats that do not. Those that do not, get holes knocked in them sooner or later.

To keep off the rocks, obey the rudder.

Obedience is not to slavishly obey this man or that, but it is that cheerful mental state which responds to the necessity of the case, and does the thing without any back talk—unuttered or expressed.

Obedience to the institution—loyalty! The man who has not learned to obey has trouble ahead of him every step of the way. The world has it in for him continually, because he has it in for the world.

The man who does not know how to receive orders is not fit to issue them to others. But the individual who knows how to execute the orders given him is preparing the way to issue orders, and better still—to have them obeyed.

Society's Saviors

All adown the ages society has made the mistake of nailing its Saviors to the cross between thieves.

That is to say, society has recognized in the Savior a very dangerous quality—something about him akin to a thief, and his career has been suddenly cut short.

We have telephones and trolly cars, yet we have not traveled far into the realm of spirit, and our X-ray has given us no insight into the heart of things.

Society is so dull and dense, so lacking in spiritual vision, so dumb and so beast-like that it does not know the difference between a thief and the only Begotten Son. In a frantic effort to forget its hollowness it takes to ping-pong, parchesi and progressive euchre, and seeks to lose itself and find solace and consolation in tiddle-dy-winks.

We are told in glaring head-lines and accurate photographic reproductions of a conference held by leaders in society to settle a matter of grave import. Was it to build technical schools and provide a means for practical and useful education? Was it a plan of building modern tenement houses along scientific and sanitary lines? Was it called to provide funds for scientific research of various kinds that would add to human knowledge and prove a benefit to mankind? No, it was none of these. This body met to determine whether the crook in a certain bulldog's tail was natural or had been produced artificially.

Should the Savior come to-day and preach the same gospel that He taught before, society would see that His experience was repeated. Now and then it blinks stupidly and cries, "Away with Him!" or it stops its game long enough to pass gall and vinegar on a spear to One it has thrust beyond the pale.

For the woman who has loved much society has but one verdict: crucify her! The best and the worst are hanged on one tree.

In the abandon of a great love there exists a godlike quality which places a woman very close to the holy of holies, yet such a one, not having complied with the edicts of society, is thrust unceremoniously forth, and society, Pilate-like, washes its hands in innocency.

Preparing for Old Age

Socrates was once asked by a pupil, this question: "What kind of people shall we be when we reach Elysium?"

And the answer was this: "We shall be the same kind of people that we were here."

If there is a life after this, we are preparing for it now, just as I am to-day preparing for my life to-morrow.

What kind of a man shall I be to-morrow? Oh, about the same kind of a man that I am now. The kind of a man that I shall be next month depends upon the kind of a man that I have been this month.

If I am miserable to-day, it is not within the round of probabilities that I shall be supremely happy to-morrow. Heaven is a habit. And if we are going to Heaven we would better be getting used to it.

Life is a preparation for the future; and the best preparation for the future is to live as if there were none.

We are preparing all the time for old age. The two things that make old age beautiful are resignation and a just consideration for the rights of others.

In the play of *Ivan the Terrible,* the interest centers around one man, the Czar Ivan. If anybody but Richard Mansfield played the part, there would be nothing in it. We simply get a glimpse into the life of a tyrant who has run the full gamut of goosedom, grumpiness, selfishness and grouch. Incidentally this man had the power to put other men to death, and this he does and has done as his whim and temper might dictate. He has been vindictive, cruel, quarrelsome, tyrannical and terrible. Now that he feels the approach of death, he would make his peace with God. But he has delayed that matter too long. He didn't realize in youth and middle life that he was then preparing for old age.

Man is the result of cause and effect, and the causes are to a degree in our hands. Life is a fluid, and well has it been called the stream of life—we are going, flowing somewhere. Strip *Ivan* of his robes and crown, and he might be an old farmer and live in Ebenezer. Every town and village has its Ivan. To be an Ivan, just turn your temper loose and practise cruelty on any person or thing within your reach, and the result will be a sure preparation for a querulous, quarrelsome, pickety, snipity, fussy and foolish old age, accented with many outbursts of wrath that are terrible in their futility and ineffectiveness.

Babyhood has no monopoly on the tantrum. The characters of *King Lear* and *Ivan the Terrible* have much in common. One might almost believe that the writer of *Ivan* had felt the incompleteness of *Lear,* and had seen the absurdity of making a melodramatic bid for sympathy in behalf of this old man thrust out by his daughters.

Lear, the troublesome, Lear to whose limber tongue there was constantly leaping words unprintable and names of tar, deserves no soft pity at our hands. All his life he had been training his three daughters for exactly the treatment he was to receive. All his life Lear had been lubricating the chute that was to give him a quick ride out into that black midnight storm.

"Oh, how sharper than a serpent's tooth it is to have a thankless child," he cries.

There is something quite as bad as a thankless child, and that is a thankless parent—an irate, irascible parent who possesses an underground vocabulary and a disposition to use it.

The false note in *Lear* lies in giving to him a daughter like *Cordelia*. Tolstoy and Mansfield ring true, and *Ivan the Terrible* is what he is without apology, excuse or explanation. Take it or leave it—if you do not like plays of this kind, go to see Vaudeville.

Mansfield's *Ivan* is terrible. The Czar is not old in years—not over seventy—but you can see that Death is sniffing close upon his track. *Ivan* has lost the power of repose. He cannot listen, weigh and decide—he has no thought or consideration for any man or thing—this is his habit of life. His bony hands are never still—the fingers open and shut, and pick at things eternally. He fumbles the cross on his breast, adjusts his jewels, scratches his cosmos, plays the devil's tattoo, gets up nervously and looks behind the throne, holds his breath to listen. When people address him, he damns them savagely if they kneel, and if they stand upright he accuses them of lack of respect. He asks that he be relieved from the cares of state, and then trembles for fear his people will take him at his word. When asked to remain ruler of Russia he proceeds to curse his councilors and accuses them of loading him with burdens that they themselves would not endeavor to bear.

He is a victim of amor senilis, and right here if Mansfield took one step more his realism would be appalling, but he stops in time and suggests what he dares not express. This tottering, doddering, slobbering, sniffling old man is in love—he is about to wed a young, beautiful girl. He selects jewels for her—he makes remarks about what would become her beauty, jeers and laughs in cracked falsetto. In the animality of youth there is something pleasing—it is natural—but the vices of an old man, when they have become only mental, are most revolting.

The people about *Ivan* are in mortal terror of him, for he is still the absolute monarch—he has the power to promote or disgrace, to take their lives or let them go free. They laugh when he laughs, cry when he does, and watch his fleeting moods with thumping hearts.

He is intensely religious and affects the robe and cowl of a priest. Around his neck hangs the crucifix. His fear is that he will die with no opportunity of confession and absolution. He prays to High Heaven every moment, kisses the cross, and his toothless old mouth interjects prayers to God and curses on man in the same breath.

If any one is talking to him he looks the other way, slips down until his shoulders occupy the throne, scratches his leg, and keeps up a running comment of insult—"Aye," "Oh," "Of course," "Certainly," "Ugh," "Listen to him now!" There is a comedy side to all this which relieves the tragedy and keeps the play from becoming disgusting.

Glimpses of *Ivan's* past are given in his jerky confessions—he is the most miserable and unhappy of men, and you behold that he is reaping as he has sown.

All his life he has been preparing for this. Each day has been a preparation for the next. *Ivan* dies in a fit of wrath, hurling curses on his family and court—dies in a fit of wrath into which he has been purposely taunted by a man who knows that the outburst is certain to kill the weakened monarch.

Where does *Ivan the Terrible* go when Death closes his eyes?

I know not. But this I believe: No confessional can absolve him—no priest benefit him—no God forgive him. He has damned himself, and he began the work in youth. He was getting ready all his life for this old age, and this old age was getting ready for the fifth act.

The playwright does not say so, Mansfield does not say so, but this is the lesson: Hate is a poison—wrath is a toxin—sensuality leads to death—clutching selfishness is a lighting of the fires of hell. It is all a preparation—cause and effect.

If you are ever absolved, you must absolve yourself, for no one else can. And the sooner you begin, the better.

We often hear of the beauties of old age, but the only old age that is beautiful is the one the man has long been preparing for by living a beautiful life. Every one of us are right now preparing for old age.

There may be a substitute somewhere in the world for Good Nature, but I do not know where it can be found.

The secret of salvation is this: Keep Sweet.

An Alliance with Nature

M‍Y FATHER is a doctor who has practised medicine for sixty-five years, and is still practising.

I am a doctor myself.

I am fifty years old; my father is eighty-five. We live in the same house, and daily we ride horseback together or tramp thru the fields and woods. To-day we did our little jaunt of five miles and back 'cross country.

I have never been ill a day—never consulted a physician in a professional way, and in fact, never missed a meal through inability to eat. As for the author of the author of *A Message to Garcia,* he holds, esoterically, to the idea that the hot pedaluvia and small doses of hop tea will cure most ailments that are curable, and so far all of his own ails have been curable—a point he can prove.

The value of the pedaluvia lies in the fact that it tends to equalize circulation, not to mention the little matter of sanitation; and the efficacy of the hops lies largely in the fact that they are bitter and disagreeable to take.

Both of these prescriptions give the patient the soothing thought that something is being done for him, and at the very worst can never do him serious harm.

My father and I are not fully agreed on all of life's themes, so existence for us never resolves itself into a dull, neutral gray. He is a Baptist and I am a Vegetarian. Occasionally he refers to me as "callow," and we have daily resorts to logic to prove prejudices, and history is searched to bolster the preconceived, but on the following important points we stand together, solid as one man:

First. Ninety-nine people out of a hundred who go to a physician have no organic disease, but are merely suffering from some symptom of their own indiscretion.

Second. Individuals who have diseases, nine times out of ten, are suffering only from the accumulated evil effects of medication.

Third. Hence we get the proposition: Most diseases are the result of medication which has been prescribed to relieve and take away a beneficent and warning symptom on the part of wise Nature.

Most of the work of doctors in the past has been to prescribe for symptoms; the difference between actual disease and a symptom being something that the average man does not even yet know.

And the curious part is that on these points all physicians, among themselves, are fully agreed. What I say here being merely truism, triteness and commonplace.

Last week, in talking with an eminent surgeon in Buffalo, he said, "I have performed over a thousand operations of laparotomy, and my records show that in every instance, excepting in cases of accident, the individual was given to what you call the 'Beecham Habit.'"

The people you see waiting in the lobbies of doctors' offices are, in a vast majority of cases, suffering thru poisoning caused by an excess of food. Coupled with this goes the bad results of imperfect breathing, irregular sleep, lack of exercise, and improper use of stimulants, or holding the thought of fear, jealousy and hate. All of these things, or any one of them, will, in very many persons, cause fever, chills, cold feet, congestion and faulty elimination.

To administer drugs to a man suffering from malnutrition caused by a desire to "get even," and a lack of fresh air, is simply to compound his troubles, shuffle his maladies, and get him ripe for the ether-cone and scalpel.

Nature is forever trying to keep people well, and most so-called "disease," which word means merely lack of ease, is self-limiting, and tends to cure itself. If you have appetite, do not eat too much. If you have no appetite, do not eat at all. Be moderate in the use of all things, save fresh air and sunshine.

The one theme of *Ecclesiastes* is moderation. Buddha wrote it down that the greatest word in any language is Equanimity. William Morris said that the finest blessing of life was systematic, useful work. Saint Paul declared that the greatest thing in the world was love. Moderation, Equanimity, Work and Love—you need no other physician.

In so stating I lay down a proposition agreed to by all physicians; which was expressed by Hippocrates, the father of medicine, and then repeated in better phrase by Epictetus, the slave, to his pupil, the great Roman Emperor, Marcus Aurelius, and which has been known to every thinking man and woman since: Moderation, Equanimity, Work and Love!

THE EX. QUESTION

WORDS sometimes become tainted and fall into bad repute, and are discarded. Until the day of Elizabeth Fry, on the official records in England appeared the word "mad-house." Then it was wiped out and the word "asylum" substituted. Within twenty years' time in several states in America we have discarded the word "asylum" and have substituted the word "hospital."

In Jeffersonville, Indiana, there is located a "Reformatory" which some years ago was known as a penitentiary. The word "prison" had a depressing effect, and "penitentiary" throws a theological shadow, and so the words will have to go. As our ideas of the criminal change, we change our vocabulary.

A few years ago we talked about asylums for the deaf and dumb—the word "dumb" has now been stricken from every official document in every state in the Union, because we have discovered, with the assistance of Gardner G. Hubbard, that deaf people are not dumb, and not being defectives, they certainly do not need an asylum. They need schools, however, and so everywhere we have established schools for the deaf.

Deaf people are just as capable, are just as competent, just as well able to earn an honest living as is the average man who can hear.

The "indeterminate sentence" is one of the wisest expedients ever brought to bear in penology. And it is to this generation alone that the honor of first using it must be given. The offender is sentenced for, say from one to eight years. This means that if the prisoner behaves himself, obeying the rules, showing a desire to be useful, he will be paroled and given his freedom at the end of one year.

If he misbehaves and does not prove his fitness for freedom he will be kept two or three years, and he may possibly have to serve the whole eight years. "How long are you in for?" I asked a convict at Jeffersonville, who was caring for the flowers in front of the walls. "Me? Oh, I'm in for two years, with the privilege of fourteen," was the man's answer, given with a grin.

The old plan of "short time," allowing two or three months off from every year for good behavior was a move in the right direction, but the indeterminate sentence will soon be the rule everywhere for first offenders.

The indeterminate sentence throws upon the man himself the responsibility for the length of his confinement and tends to relieve prison life of its horror, by holding out hope. The man has the short time constantly in mind, and usually is very careful not to do anything to imperil it. Insurrection and an attempt to escape may mean that every day of the whole long sentence will have to be served.

So even the dullest of minds and the most calloused realize that it pays to do what is right—the lesson being pressed home upon them in a way it has never been before.

The old-time prejudice of business men against the man who had "done time" was chiefly on account of his incompetence, and not his record. The prison methods that turned out a hateful, depressed and frightened man who had been suppressed by the silent system and deformed by the lock-step, calloused by brutal treatment and the constant thought held over him that he was a criminal, was a bad thing for the prisoner, for the keeper and for society. Even an upright man would be undone by such treatment, and in a year be transformed into a sly, secretive and morally sick man. The men just out of prison were unable to do anything—they needed constant supervision and attention, and so of course we did not care to hire them.

The Ex. now is a totally different man from the Ex. just out of his striped suit in the seventies, thanks to that much defamed man, Brockway, and a few others.

We may have to restrain men for the good of themselves and the good of society, but we do not punish. The restraint is punishment enough; we believe men are punished by their sins, not for them.

When men are sent to reform schools now, the endeavor and the hope is to give back to society a better man than we took.

Judge Lindsey sends boys to the reform school without officer or guard. The boys go of their own accord, carrying their own commitment papers. They pound on the gate demanding admittance in the name of the law.

The boy believes that Judge Lindsey is his friend, and that the reason he is sent to the reform school is that he may reap a betterment which his full freedom cannot possibly offer. When he takes his commitment papers he is no longer at war with society and the keepers of the law. He believes that what is being done for him is done for the best, and so he goes to prison, which is really not a prison at the last, for it is a school where the lad is taught to economize both time and money and to make himself useful.

Other people work for us, and we must work for them. This is the supreme lesson that the boy learns. You can only help yourself by helping others.

Now here is a proposition: If a boy or a man takes his commitment papers, goes to prison alone and unattended, is it necessary that he should be there locked up, enclosed in a corral and be looked after by guards armed with death-dealing implements?

Superintendent Whittaker, of the institution at Jeffersonville, Indiana, says, "No." He believes that within ten years' time we will do away with the high wall, and will keep our loaded guns out of sight; to a great degree also we will take the bars from the windows of the prisons, just as we have taken them away from the windows of the hospitals for the insane.

At the reform school it may be necessary to have a guard-house for some years to come, but the high wall must go, just as we have sent the lock-step and the silent system and the striped suit of disgrace into the ragbag of time—lost in the memory of things that were.

Four men out of five in the reformatory at Jeffersonville need no coercion, they would not run away if the walls were razed and the doors left unlocked. One young man I saw there refused the offered parole—he wanted to stay until he learned his trade. He was not the only one with a like mental attitude.

The quality of men in the average prison is about the same as that of the men who are in the United States Army. The man who enlists is a prisoner; for him to run away is a very serious offense, and yet he is not locked up at night, nor is he surrounded by a high wall.

The George Junior Republic is simply a farm, unfenced and unpatroled, excepting by the boys who are in the Republic, and yet it is a penal institution. The prison of the future will not be unlike a young ladies' boarding school, where even yet the practice prevails of taking the inmates out all together, with a guard, and allowing no one to leave without a written permit.

As society changes, so changes the so-called criminal. In any event, I know this—that Max Nordau did not make out his case.

There is no criminal class.

Or for that matter we are all criminals. "I have in me the capacity for every crime," said Emerson.

The man or woman who goes wrong is a victim of unkind environment. Booker Washington says that when the negro has something that we want, or can perform a task that we want done, we waive the color line, and the race problem then ceases to be a problem. So it is with the Ex. Question. When the ex-convict is able to show that he is useful to the world, the world will cease to shun him. When Superintendent Whittaker graduates a man it is pretty good evidence that the man is able and willing to render a service to society.

The only places where the ex-convicts get the icy mitt are pink teas and prayer meetings. An ex-convict should work all day and then spend his evenings at the library, feeding his mind—then he is safe.

If I were an ex-convict I would fight shy of all "Refuges," "Sheltering Arms," "Saint Andrew's Societies" and the philanthropic "College Settlements." I would never go to those good professional people, or professional good people, who patronize the poor and spit upon the alleged wrongdoer, and who draw sharp lines of demarcation in distinguishing between the "good" and the "bad." If you can work and are willing to work, business men will not draw the line on you. Get a job, and then hold it down hard by making yourself necessary. Employers of labor and the ex-convicts themselves are fast settling this Ex. Question, with the help of the advanced type of the Reform School where the inmates are being taught to be useful and are not punished nor patronized, but are simply given a chance. My heart goes out in sympathy to the man who gives a poor devil a chance. I myself am a poor devil!

The Sergeant

A COLONEL in the United States Army told me the other day something like this: The most valuable officer, the one who has the greatest responsibility, is the sergeant. The true sergeant is born, not made—he is the priceless gift of the gods. He is so highly prized that when found he is never promoted, nor is he allowed to resign. If he is dissatisfied with his pay, Captain, Lieutenant and Colonel chip in—they cannot afford to lose him. He is a rara avis—the apple of their eye.

His first requirement is that he must be able to lick any man in the company. A drunken private may damn a captain upside down and wrong-side out, and the captain is not allowed to reply. He can neither strike with his fist, nor engage in a cussing match, but your able sergeant is an adept in both of these polite accomplishments. Even if a private strike an officer, the officer is not allowed to strike back. Perhaps the man who abuses him could easily beat him in a rough-and-tumble fight, and then it is quite a sufficient reason to keep one's clothes clean. We say the revolver equalizes all men, but it doesn't. It is disagreeable to shoot a man. It scatters brains and blood all over the sidewalk, attracts a crowd, requires a deal of explanation afterward, and may cost an officer his stripes. No good officer ever hears anything said about him by a private.

The sergeant hears everything, and his reply to back-slack is a straight-arm jab in the jaw. The sergeant is responsible only to his captain, and no good captain will ever know anything about what a sergeant does, and he will not believe it when told. If a fight occurs between two privates, the sergeant jumps in, bumps their heads together and licks them both. If a man feigns sick, or is drunk, the sergeant chucks him under the pump. The regulations do not call for any such treatment, but the sergeant does not know anything about the regulations—he gets the thing done. The sergeant may be twenty years old or sixty—age does not count. The sergeant is a father to his men—he regards them all as children—bad boys—and his business is to make them brave, honorable and dutiful soldiers.

The sergeant is always the first man up in the morning, the last man to go to bed at night. He knows where his men are every minute of the day or night. If they are actually sick, he is both nurse and physician, and dictates gently to the surgeon what should be done. He is also the undertaker, and the digging of ditches and laying out of latrines all fall to his lot. Unlike the higher officers, he does not have to dress "smart," and he is very apt to discard his uniform and go clothed like a civilian teamster, excepting on special occasions when necessity demands braid and buttons.

He knows everything, and nothing. No wild escapade of a higher officer passes by him, yet he never tells.

Now one might suppose that he is an absolute tyrant, but a good sergeant is a beneficent tyrant at the right time. To break the spirit of his men will not do—it would unfit them for service—so what he seeks to do is merely to bend their minds so as to match his own. Gradually they grow to both love and fear him. In time of actual fight he transforms cowards into heroes. He holds his men up to the scratch. In battle there are often certain officers marked for death—they are to be shot by their own men. It is a time of getting even—and in the hurly-burly and excitement there are no witnesses. The sergeant is ever on the lookout for such mutinies, and his revolver often sends to the dust the head revolutionary before the dastardly plot can be carried out. In war-time all executions are not judicial.

In actual truth, the sergeant is the only real, sure-enough fighting man in the army. He is as rare as birds' teeth, and every officer anxiously scans his recruits in search of good sergeant timber.

In business life, the man with the sergeant instincts is even more valuable than in the army. The business sergeant is the man not in evidence—who asks for no compliments or bouquets—who knows where things are—who has no outside ambitions, and no desire save to do his work. If he is too smart he will lay plots and plans for his own promotion, and thereby he is pretty sure to defeat himself.

As an individual the average soldier is a sneak, a shirk, a failure, a coward. He is only valuable as he is licked into shape. It is pretty much the same in business. It seems hard to say it, but the average employe in factory, shop or store, puts the face of the clock to shame looking at it; he is thinking of his pay envelope and his intent is to keep the boss located and to do as little work as possible. In many cases the tyranny of the employer is to blame for the condition, but more often it is the native outcrop of suspicion that prompts the seller to give no more than he can help.

And here the sergeant comes in, and with watchful eye and tireless nerves, holds the recreants to their tasks. If he is too severe, he will fix in the shirks more firmly the shirk microbe; but if he is of better fibre, he may supply a little more will to those who lack it, and gradually create an atmosphere of right intent, so that the only disgrace will consist in their wearing the face off the regulator and keeping one ear cocked to catch the coming footsteps of the boss.

There is not the slightest danger that there will ever be an overplus of sergeants. Let the sergeant keep out of strikes, plots, feuds, hold his temper and show what's what, and he can name his own salary and keep his place for ninety-nine years without having a contract.

The Spirit of the Age

Four hundred and twenty-five years before the birth of the Nazarene, Socrates said, "The gods are on high Olympus, but you and I are here." And for this—and a few other similar observations—be was compelled to drink a substitute for coffee—he was an infidel! Within the last thirty years the churches of Christendom have, in the main, adopted the Socratic proposition that you and I are here. That is, we have made progress by getting away from narrow theology and recognizing humanity. We do not know anything about either Olympus or Elysium, but we do know something about Athens.

Athens is here.

Athens needs us—the Greeks are at the door. Let the gods run Elysium, and we'll devote ourselves to Athens.

This is the prevailing spirit in the churches of America to-day. Our religion is humanitarian, not theological.

A like evolution has come about in medicine. The materia medica of twenty-five years ago is now obsolete. No good doctor now treats symptoms—he neither gives you something to relieve your headache nor to settle your stomach. These are but timely ting-a-lings—Nature's warnings—look out! And the doctor tells you so, and charges you a fee sufficient to impress you with the fact that he is no fool, but that you are.

The lawyer who now gets the largest fees is never seen in a court-room. Litigation is now largely given over to damage suits—carried on by clients who want something for nothing, and little lawyers, shark-like and hungry, who work on contingent fees. Three-fourths of the time of all superior and supreme courts is taken up by His Effluvia, who brings suit thru His Bacteria, with His Crabship as chief witness, for damages not due, either in justice or fact.

How to get rid of this burden, brought upon us by men who have nothing to lose, is a question too big for the average legislator. It can only be solved by heroic measures, carried out by lawyers who are out of politics and have a complete indifference for cheap popularity. Here is opportunity for men of courage and ability. But the point is this, wise business men keep out of court. They arbitrate their differences —compromise—they cannot afford to quit their work for the sake of getting even. As for making money, they know a better way.

In theology we are waiving distinctions and devoting ourselves to the divine spirit only as it manifests itself in humanity—we are talking less and less about another world and taking more notice of the one we inhabit. Of course we occasionally have heresy trials, and pictures of the offender and the Fat Bishop adorn the first page, but heresy trials not accompanied by the scaffold or the faggots are innocuous and exceedingly tame.

In medicine we have more faith in ourselves and less in prescriptions.

In pedagogy we are teaching more and more by the natural method—learning by doing—and less and less by means of injunction and precept.

In penology we seek to educate and reform, not to suppress, repress and punish.

That is to say, the gods are on high Olympus—let them stay there. Athens is here.

The Grammarian

The best way to learn to write is to write.

Herbert Spencer never studied grammar until he had learned to write. He took his grammar at sixty, which is a good age for one to begin this most interesting study, as by the time you have reached that age you have largely lost your capacity to sin.

Men who can swim exceedingly well are not those who have taken courses in the theory of swimming at natatoriums, from professors of the amphibian art—they were just boys who jumped into the ol' swimmin' hole, and came home with shirts on wrong-side out and a tell-tale dampness in their hair.

Correspondence schools for the taming of bronchos are as naught; and treatises on the gentle art of wooing are of no avail—follow nature's lead.

Grammar is the appendenda vermiformis of the science of pedagogics: it is as useless as the letter q in the alphabet, or the proverbial two tails to a cat, which no cat ever had, and the finest cat in the world, the Manx cat, has no tail at all.

"The literary style of most university men is commonplace, when not positively bad," wrote Herbert Spencer in his old age.

"Educated Englishmen all write alike," said Taine. That is to say, educated men who have been drilled to write by certain fixed and unchangeable rules of rhetoric and grammar will produce similar compositions. They have no literary style, for style is individuality and character—the style is the man, and grammar tends to obliterate individuality. No study is so irksome to everybody, except the sciolists who teach it, as grammar. It remains forever a bad taste in the mouth of the man of ideas, and has weaned bright minds innumerable from a desire to express themselves through the written word.

Grammar is the etiquette of words, and the man who does not know how to properly salute his grandmother on the street until he has consulted a book, is always so troubled about the tenses that his fancies break thru language and escape.

The grammarian is one whose whole thought is to string words according to a set formula. The substance itself that he wishes to convey is of secondary importance. Orators who keep their thoughts upon the proper way to gesticulate in curves, impress nobody.

If it were a sin against decency, or an attempt to poison the minds of the people, for a person to be ungrammatical, it might be wise enough to hire men to protect the well of English from defilement. But a stationary language is a dead one—moving water only is pure—

and the well that is not fed by springs is sure to be a breeding-place for disease.

Let men express themselves in their own way, and if they express themselves poorly, look you, their punishment will be that no one will read their literary effusions. Oblivion with her smother-blanket lies in wait for the writer who has nothing to say and says it faultlessly.

In the making of hare soup, I am informed by most excellent culinary authority, the first requisite is to catch your hare. The literary scullion who has anything to offer a hungry world, will doubtless find a way to fricassee it.

The Best Religion

A RELIGION of just being kind would be a pretty good religion, don't you think so?

But a religion of kindness and useful effort is nearly a perfect religion.

We used to think it was a man's belief concerning a dogma that would fix his place in eternity. This was because we believed that God was a grumpy, grouchy old gentleman, stupid, touchy and dictatorial. A really good man would not damn you even if you didn't like him, but a bad man would.

As our ideas of God changed, we ourselves changed for the better. Or, as we thought better of ourselves we thought better of God. It will be character that locates our place in another world, if there is one, just as it is our character that fixes our place here.

We are weaving character every day, and the way to weave the best character is to be kind and to be useful.

>THINK RIGHT, ACT RIGHT; IT IS WHAT WE THINK AND DO THAT MAKE US WHAT WE ARE.